101

GREAT

Games
&
Activities

Edited by
Arthur VanGundy, Ph.D.

Pfeiffer
A Wiley Imprint
www.pfeiffer.com

Published by Pfeiffer
A Wiley Imprint
One Montgomery Street, Suite 1200, San Francisco, CA 94104-4594
www.pfeiffer.com

For additional copies/bulk purchases of this book in the U.S. please contact 800-274-4434.

Pfeiffer books and products are available through most bookstores. To contact Pfeiffer directly call our Customer Care Department within the U.S. at 800-274-4434, outside the U.S. at 317-572-3985, fax 317-572-4002, or visit www.pfeiffer.com.

Pfeiffer Wiley also publishes its books in a variety of electronic formats and by print-on-demand. Some material included with standard print versions of this book may not be included in e-books or in print-on-demand. If the version of this book that you purchased references media such as a CD or DVD that was not included in your purchase, you may download this material at http://booksupport.wiley.com. For more information about Wiley products, visit www.wiley.com.

ISBN: 978-0-7879-4138-3 (loose-leaf); ISBN: 978-1-118-29601-1 (paper)

Acquiring Editor:	Matt Holt
Director of Development:	Kathleen Dolan Davies
Developmental Editor:	Rebecca Taff
Senior Production Editor:	Dawn Kilgore
Illustrations:	Dovetail Publishing Services

PB Printing 10 9 8 7 6 5 4 3 2 1

Dedication

To
My daughters Sarah and Laura
and my future grandchild

Table of Contents

Preface

Corporate downsizing and across-the-board resource reductions often result in cutbacks in training budgets and programs. The need for training during such times, however, assumes increasing importance. Fewer employees must do more with less. To slight training is to risk not achieving performance objectives.

An ever-sophisticated work force demands new approaches to training and new training activities. One of my primary objectives in editing this book was to provide trainers with previously unpublished activities. Although some may have circulated among informal training networks, all the contributors were asked to submit original, unpublished work.

The activities are organized into twenty different categories, representing a variety of training topics. They range from icebreakers, climate-setting, and getting-acquainted activities to diversity, team-building, evaluation, and implementation activities. The differing backgrounds of the contributors add variety that is not possible when activities are written by one or two authors alone.

To help you, the reader, select from among activities, I have prepared a decision matrix, which follows this preface. The activities are listed alphabetically down the left side of the matrix; categories of usage are listed across the top. As with any categorization scheme, there is some overlap among categories. An activity in the leadership category, for instance, also may be useful for climate setting and team building. The alternative uses of each exercise are designated by an "X" in the grid. Thus, the Broomstick Demonstration has "Xs" under the topical headings for "Icebreaker" and "Team Building." The small rectangle indicates where the activity is located in the book. Thus, for the Broomstick Demonstration example, the rectangle appears under the category of "Change Management."

I am indebted to all the contributors who helped make this book possible. I cannot list all of their names here, but a complete listing, with short biographies and information for contacting them, is at the end of this book. Thank you all for your contributions.

Finally, I would like to acknowledge the highly professional, invaluable, and friendly support and encouragement I received from the editors at Jossey-Bass/Pfeiffer: Kathleen Dolan Davies, Dawn Kilgore, Rebecca Taff, Josh Blatter, and especially Matt Holt who originally contacted me and helped me "hatch" the overall concept and its structure. Their personal contact and attention to detail made it a pleasure to work with them.

I hope you, the reader, find this book useful. I would be happy to receive any feedback whatsoever about it. Or, if you have any activities you would like to submit for possible future volumes of this work, please e-mail them to me at avangundy@aol.com or fax them to me at 405-447-1960.

Decision Matrix for Selecting Activities

Activity	Career Development	Change Management	Clarifying Expectations	Climate Setting	Communication	Creativity	Diversity	Energizers	Evaluation	Getting to Know You	Goal Setting	Icebreakers	Implementation	Interviewing	Leadership	Listening	Negotiation	Problem Solving	Team Building	Values
Baptism by Fire														□					X	
Been There, Said That				X	X	□										□		X		
Belt It Out		X		X												X		X		
Benchmarking Team Feelings				X					□										X	
Bond and Connect				□X	X			□											X	
Box of Life																				X
Boxes of Your Life			X	X		X													X	
Broomstick Demonstration												X	□						X	
Cartoon Time								X		□		X								
Comic Relief				X	X			X		□		X								
Composition				X	X												X		□	
Corporate Jester				X		X						□								X
Creating Aim												□							X	X

Key: □ = Original topic used to classify the activity.
X = Activity also appropriate for designated topic.

Decision Matrix for Selecting Activities

Key: □ = Original topic used to classify the activity. X = Activity also appropriate for designated topic.

Activity	Career Development	Change Management	Clarifying Expectations	Climate Setting	Communication	Creativity	Diversity	Energizers	Evaluation	Getting to Know You	Goal Setting	Icebreakers	Implementation	Interviewing	Leadership	Listening	Negotiation	Problem Solving	Team Building	Values
Divided or Diversified?							□	X				X							X	
Do You Hear What I Play?					□ X											X	X		X	
Empowered to Know				□									X	□					X	
Excuuuse Me!					X								X						□	
Feather Talk					X	X											X		X	
Five Double You's									X		X							X	X	
Follow the Word Leader													□		□				X	
Get on the Soapbox				X		X		X			□								□	
Goal Pictures								□											X	
Go Team! RAH!				X								X							X	
Group Interviewing Criteria			□											□					X	
Guaranteed to Fail				X		X		X		X									X	X
Hands-On Networking								□				X							X	

101 Great Games & Activities. Copyright © 1998 by John Wiley & Sons, Inc.
Reproduced by permission of Pfeiffer, an Imprint of Wiley. www.pfeiffer.com

Decision Matrix for Selecting Activities

Key: □ = Original topic used to classify the activity.
X = Activity also appropriate for designated topic.

Activity	Career Development	Change Management	Clarifying Expectations	Climate Setting	Communication	Creativity	Diversity	Energizers	Evaluation	Getting to Know You	Goal Setting	Icebreakers	Implementation	Interviewing	Leadership	Listening	Negotiation	Problem Solving	Team Building	Values
Handshaking				X		X		X				□							X	
Helping Others Deal with Change		□													X				X	
How to Win Over the Boss	X				X	X										X	□			
Hugs and Kisses				X				□				X								
I Believe					X	X	□													X
I Never Thought of It That Way!					X	X														
Identifying Cultural Assumptions					X	X	X											□	X	□
Incredible Difficulty of Communicating Simple Ideas					□															
Influence, Not Authority					□	X							X		X	X			X	
It All Depends						X									□	X			X	
It Just Doesn't Add Up					X	□												X		
It's a Man's World After All					X	X	□													X

Decision Matrix for Selecting Activities

Activity	Career Development	Change Management	Clarifying Expectations	Climate Setting	Communication	Creativity	Diversity	Energizers	Evaluation	Getting to Know You	Goal Setting	Icebreakers	Implementation	Interviewing	Leadership	Listening	Negotiation	Problem Solving	Team Building	Values
It's Crystal Clear to Me			X	X	□											X				
KNOWU Cards				X				X		X		□								
Language Bias					□		X									X			X	
Leadership Inventory						X		X				X			□				X	
Let's Connect!				X		X				□		X								
Let's Get to Know One Another				X		X				□		X								
Light, Medium, or Heavy				X			□			□		X							X	
Lobbying		X			X	X											□			
Mandalas				X		X				X		X				X			X	
Meet and Greet				X	X			□												X
Mental Rehearsal						□							□							
More Ideas Than You!																		X	X	
More Similar Than Different							X										□	X	X	

Key: □ = Original topic used to classify the activity.
X = Activity also appropriate for designated topic.

101 Great Games & Activities. Copyright © 1998 by John Wiley & Sons, Inc.
Reproduced by permission of Pfeiffer, an Imprint of Wiley. www.pfeiffer.com

Decision Matrix for Selecting Activities

Activity	Career Development	Change Management	Clarifying Expectations	Climate Setting	Communication	Creativity	Diversity	Energizers	Evaluation	Getting to Know You	Goal Setting	Icebreakers	Implementation	Interviewing	Leadership	Listening	Negotiation	Problem Solving	Team Building	Values
More Than One Way to Skin a Question				X										□					X	
Music Machine	□			X		X	□	X											X	
Myths										X									X	
New Hires						X		X			□							X	X	
Objects	□					X									X				X	
Occupational Grab Bag	□					X				X		X							X	
Perceptions				□								X							X	
Personal Mission Statement									□		□								X	X
Phrase Phases			X			X				□									X	
Picture That				X		X			□			X								
Pieces of the Puzzle			X		X						X								X	
Pipe Cleaner Challenge					X	X												□		

Key: □ = Original topic used to classify the activity.
X = Activity also appropriate for designated topic.

Decision Matrix for Selecting Activities

Activity	Career Development	Change Management	Clarifying Expectations	Climate Setting	Communication	Creativity	Diversity	Energizers	Evaluation	Getting to Know You	Goal Setting	Icebreakers	Implementation	Interviewing	Leadership	Listening	Negotiation	Problem Solving	Team Building	Values
Problem as Solution to Another Problem						X												□		
Promoting and Selling Ideas		X			X	□									X		X	X		
Puzzling	□		X	X		X						X			X					
Relationship Map				X						□									□	
Road Maps		X		X								X			X				X	
Role Observation Illumination								X											□	
Rumperstickers				□				X		X		X								
Sandwich to Go						X		X					□					X		
Saucy Deal					X	X	X									□	□			
Say What?					X													X	X	
Secret Coaches				X		X		X							X				□	
Showing What We Have Learned								X	□										X	
Six Pack				X				X		X									□	

Key: □ = Original topic used to classify the activity.
X = Activity also appropriate for designated topic.

Decision Matrix for Selecting Activities

Activity	Career Development	Change Management	Clarifying Expectations	Climate Setting	Communication	Creativity	Diversity	Energizers	Evaluation	Getting to Know You	Goal Setting	Icebreakers	Implementation	Interviewing	Leadership	Listening	Negotiation	Problem Solving	Team Building	Values
S.M.A.R.T. Basketball									x		□							x	x	
Stand by Me		x						x	□			x						x	x	
Taking Charge														□					x	
Taking Ownership of New Ideas				x	x	x								□						
Talking Stick				x	x			x	x	x		x				□	x		x	
That's the Worst Idea I've Ever Heard!					x	□														
The Tie That Binds			□	x				x				x							x	
There Must Be a Leader in This Group				x				x				x			□	x		x	x	
Things That Rhyme					x	x						x						□	x	
Think About It						□							x					x	x	
Tri-Counseling													x	□					x	x
Tripping				x		□												x		

Key: □ = Original topic used to classify the activity.
x = Activity also appropriate for designated topic.

Decision Matrix for Selecting Activities

Activity	Career Development	Change Management	Clarifying Expectations	Climate Setting	Communication	Creativity	Diversity	Energizers	Evaluation	Getting to Know You	Goal Setting	Icebreakers	Implementation	Interviewing	Leadership	Listening	Negotiation	Problem Solving	Team Building	Values
Turning Misery into Merriment		□										X							X	
Under the Sea				X		X	□	X												
Value Valuation					X	X	X												X	□
Values Roll Call							X											X		□
Valuing Diversity					X		□													X
Vanity Plates				□		X		X		X		X			X					
Wall Murals			□	X						X										
We've Got Rhythm			□	X						X									X	
What's My Line?				X						X		X								
Who Are These People?				X						□		X							X	
Whole-Brain Learning						X												□		
Why? Why? Why?							X					X							X	□
Will We or Won't We?					X											X				

Key: □ = Original topic used to classify the activity. X = Activity also appropriate for designated topic.

Career Development

Myths

Objectives

- To identify myths from childhood that have implications in adulthood
- To examine childhood myths as they affect adult beliefs and behaviors
- To demonstrate that people share common experiences

Uses

This activity is useful to help individuals understand how their early childhood experiences might affect their current views, expectations, and behavior. It is not intended to be any type of valid psychological analysis and should be kept on the light side. The activity can also be used for getting acquainted.

Audience

All levels

Time

Sixty minutes

Handouts, Materials, and Equipment

- Paper and pencils for all participants
- A flip chart and markers

Procedure

1. Ask the participants to think of a myth or fairy tale that they identified with in childhood.
2. Give them paper and pencils and have each of them spend ten minutes writing a paragraph on the impact that the myth or fairy tale had on their young lives.
3. Divide the group into pairs or trios and ask them to share what they have written with one another for about ten minutes.

4. Now give the pairs or trios twenty minutes to discuss with one another how any of what they have written may have carried over into adulthood and their careers, answering the following questions:

How might these myths or fairy tales have influenced your choice of career?

What differences and/or similarities in reactions or feelings have you experienced later in your life as a result of reading the fairy tale or myth as a child?

Has the influence been positive or negative overall?

Discussion

Bring everyone together in the large group for about twenty minutes; ask for volunteers to share what some of their discoveries were. Write some common thoughts that emerge on the flip chart. Discuss the differences between what they thought as children and what actually happened in their lives.

Variation

Use a movie star or cartoon character instead of a myth or fairy tale.

Source
Doris J. Shallcross

Objects

Objectives

- To help people gain insight into their careers
- To encourage people to take career risks

Uses

This activity can be used for career-development training, team building, or as an exercise in risk taking.

Audience

Small groups of people who are at mid-career

Time

Sixty minutes

Handouts, Materials, and Equipment

- A flip chart and paper for each subgroup
- Markers for each subgroup
- Two different objects for each subgroup, one representing something "safe" (e.g., a towel, pillow, or eraser) and one representing something "dangerous" (e.g., a razor blade, knife, or a pair of scissors)

Procedure

1. Divide participants into subgroups of three or four and give each subgroup one "safe" object and one "dangerous" object. (*Note:* Each subgroup should have a different object.)

2. Give each subgroup a flip chart and markers and ask them to spend fifteen minutes examining their "safe" objects and listing all the characteristics and features it has on the flip chart, e.g., soft, fluffy, supportive, lightweight, uses a slipcover, comfortable to sleep on, or colorful.

3. When they have finished, instruct each group to spend fifteen minutes describing all the characteristics and features of the "dangerous" object, e.g., sharp, metallic, thin, used to cut, needs sharpening, or comes in different sizes.

4. Now have the individual group members use descriptive words from their lists to write sentences about times they have taken the "safe" route in their careers; for instance, "One of my jobs was kind of 'fluffy' because I really didn't have that much work to do" or "I was able to 'cover up' my lack of experience and get by." Give them five minutes to write down several responses.

5. Next have the individual group members use descriptive words from their lists to write sentences about times they have taken the "dangerous" route during their careers; for instance, "I cut some corners to save money and could have lost my job if they'd found out." Give them five minutes to write down several responses.

Discussion

Ask the participants to discuss their reactions to the activity. Ask questions such as:

How do you feel about some of the "safe" choices you have made in your career?

How do you feel about some of the "dangerous" choices you have made in your career?

What did you learn from looking back at your choices?

Could you have taken more chances?

How can you use this information to plan the rest of your career?

Variation

The topic can be changed to focus on a particular training area such as leadership or creativity.

Source
Arthur VanGundy

Occupational Grab Bag

Objectives

- To explore career-development opportunities
- To help participants assess their career strengths and weaknesses

Uses

The activity can be used for career development or general team building.

Audience

Any level, any size group

Time

Thirty to sixty minutes, depending on group size

Handouts, Materials, and Equipment

- At least five sheets of paper for each participant
- Pens or pencils for participants
- One *Occupational Grab Bag Job Titles List* for each participant

Procedure

1. Distribute one copy of the *Occupational Grab Bag Job Titles List,* five sheets of paper, and a pen or pencil to each participant. Read the instructions on the handout aloud to the group, asking them to follow along.

2. When everyone has finished, ask them to write the four job titles they have chosen (favorable or not) at the top center of the sheets of paper, one per sheet, and to draw a vertical line down the center of the paper under the job title. Tell them to label the left-hand column "Strengths" and the right-hand column "Weaknesses." Draw an example for them, if necessary.

3. Tell them to write down at least five abilities that they possess that would be either strengths (left-hand column) or weaknesses (right-hand column) for each of these occupations. Give as an example: "If you selected the occupation of Doll Maker, a

strength might be your ability to come up with a lot of creative designs; a weakness might be your inability to sew."

4. When they have finished, ask them to examine their strengths and weaknesses for each of the occupations they have listed and to use these to brainstorm ways to improve their *current* jobs or careers. Give as an example: "The ability to devise creative doll designs might prompt you to think of incorporating more creative activities on the job or possibly a career shift into a more creative occupation. The weakness of not being able to sew might suggest delegating more activities or 'stitching together' your own consulting group and leaving the corporate world." Be sure that everyone is clear on what to do and then give them about fifteen minutes.

5. Now tell participants to devise action plans to implement their new ideas. Be sure that they include a time frame, obstacles they may encounter, and ways to overcome the obstacles. Tell them to use the blank sheet of paper for writing their plans.

Discussion

To help participants focus on the next steps in their careers, ask the following questions:

What new insights did you gain about your job or career?

Did you gain more ideas from the "strengths" or from the "weaknesses"? Why?

What would you do differently in your career if you had the chance to start over again?

Are there any weaknesses you had earlier in your career that now are strengths?

Do job or career strengths vary in importance depending on the job? Can a strength in one job be a weakness in another or vice versa? Why?

Variations

1. Have small groups form and share their responses.
2. Use the responses from all participants to devise a general strategy for career development.

Source
Arthur VanGundy

Occupational Grab Bag Job Titles List

Instructions: Look over the list of occupational titles below. Select two (other than your own) that appeal to you and two that you would *not* like to do (you may also write in occupations not on the list). When you are finished, wait for further instructions.

Accountant	Actor	Ambassador
Architect	Artist	Astronaut
Athlete	Attorney	Auditor
Baker	Bricklayer	Bus Driver
Business Executive	Butcher	Butler
Cab Driver	Cabinetmaker	Candlestick Maker
Carpenter	Cleaner	Clerk
Coach	Computer Programmer	Cook
Copywriter	Counselor	Cowboy/Cowgirl
Dancer	Dentist	Dishwasher
Doll Maker	Editor	Electrician
Engineer	Farmer	Fashion Designer
Flight Attendant	Garbage Collector	Glassblower
Grave Digger	Janitor	Machinist
Maid	Mason	Minister/Priest/Rabbi
Musician	Nurse	Pharmacist
Philosopher	Physicist	Physician
Professor	Pilot	Potter
Psychologist	Real Estate Broker	Researcher
Rocket Scientist	Salesperson	Secretary
Shoemaker	Soldier (Military)	Stockbroker
Tailor	Teacher	Telephone Operator
Therapist	Travel Agent	Truck Driver
Undertaker	Waiter/Waitress	Welder
Writer		

Road Maps

Objectives

- To help people explore their past, present, and future careers
- To help people find common past experiences or future desires

Uses

This activity can be used for career-development training, as an icebreaker for team building, or to build trust among members of a team in conflict.

Audience

Small groups from existing or newly-formed teams

Time

Ninety minutes

Handouts, Materials, and Equipment

- A flip chart with enough sheets of paper for each participant
- A variety of colored markers for each participant
- Paper and pencils for each participant
- One copy of the *Road Map Sample Handout* for each participant

Procedure

1. Hand out paper and pencils and instruct the participants to write down their answers to the following questions individually. (*Note:* You may wish to write them on the flip chart prior to the session.)

   Where were you born and raised?

   Who were your childhood friends?

   What were your favorite childhood games?

   What did you do especially well?

   Which adults had the most influence on your life?

What was your first job?

What did you like about it? Dislike about it?

What are some other jobs you have held?

What were your favorite jobs and why?

What jobs did you dislike and why?

What have been your major career accomplishments? Why do you consider them to be so?

What have you been least proud of in your career? Why?

How happy are you with the direction your career has taken to this point, on a scale of one to ten?

What career goals do you have for one year from now? Three years? Five years?

What would your "dream job" be like?

What do you want to do when you retire?

2. After everyone has finished (about fifteen minutes), distribute a variety of colored markers to the participants and give each person a sheet of flip-chart paper.

3. Give everyone a copy of the *Road Map Sample Handout.* Tell the group that each of them will create a road map of his or her own career based on reflections of the past and hopes for the future that each of them has written on the papers. Post the following ground rules:

   • Use pictures only (no words).

   • Use at least five different colors.

   • You have thirty minutes.

   • Start at the beginning of your career and continue through retirement.

   • Have fun with this activity.

4. Call time after thirty minutes and have participants post their road maps in the "Art Gallery" for viewing. (*Note:* The facilitator may wish to create a road map of his or her own career and post it also.)

5. Ask each "artist" to explain his or her road map briefly to the rest of the group and to autograph the piece, just as any artist would do. Allow approximately five minutes per artist for sharing and autographing.

Discussion

Ask the participants to discuss their reactions to the activity. Ask questions such as:

   How did it feel to make a road map of your career?

   What did you learn from your road map?

   What did you learn about others from their road maps?

   How can you use this information to plan the rest of your career?

Variation

The topic can be changed from a focus on career to a particular aspect of training, such as leadership or creativity.

Source
Frank Prince

Road Map Sample Handout

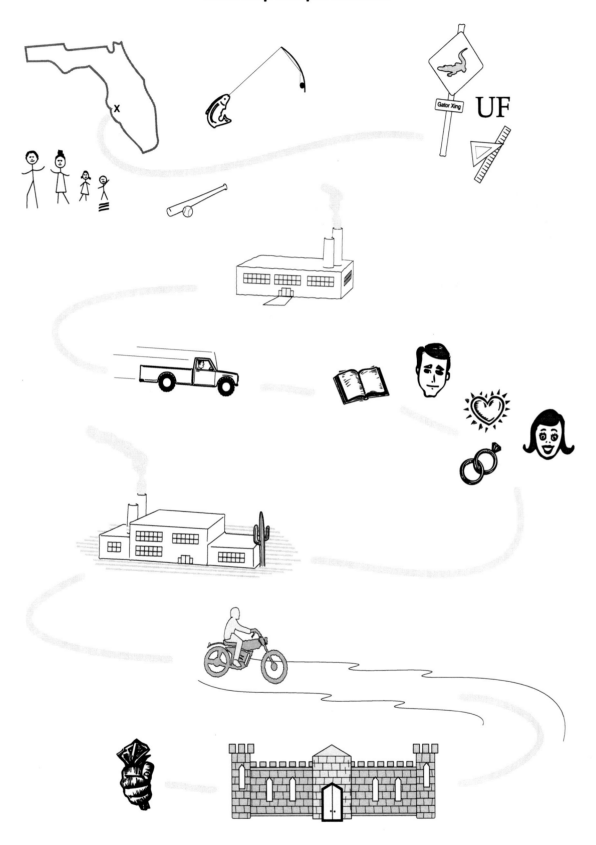

Change Management

Broomstick Demonstration

Objectives

- To provide an example of Lewin's Force Field Analysis
- To help participants see the differences between driving and restraining forces
- To facilitate overcoming or weakening restraining forces in order to reach a desired state

Uses

This exercise is for general change management or leadership training.

Time

Approximately thirty minutes

Audience

Any size and level

Handouts, Materials, and Equipment

- A broomstick or pole
- Masking tape
- A flip chart and markers
- An overhead projector
- An overhead transparency of *Broomstick Force Field Analysis Example*
- Copies of *Broomstick Force Field Practice* for each participant.
- Copies of *Broomstick Exercise: Creating a Force Field Analysis* and *Broomstick Debriefing* for each participant

Procedure

1. Choose six volunteers from the group to participate in a demonstration of Force Field Analysis. Say in a teasing way that the volunteers will not play speaking parts, but that there will be some physical activity involved and that only the strong

and healthy will survive. Play up the strength and confidence characteristics required of volunteers.

2. Divide the volunteers into two groups of three and put one group on each side of a broomstick with their hands on the stick. Try to divide the groups so that they are balanced in terms of height, strength, and weight. One group represents the "Driving Forces" and the other group the "Restraining Forces." Have them remain in place at the front of the room.

3. Show the *Broomstick Force Field Analysis Example* on the overhead projector and explain the importance of Driving Forces in change. Point out that Restraining Forces and Driving Forces are adversarial and that they push against one another. This tension holds the person or organization in its present state.

4. Tell the participants to imagine that they are volunteers in an organization that is seeking change, in which the Driving Forces represent the employees responsible for bringing about the change. Tape a strip of masking tape about five feet long on the floor several feet behind the Restraining Forces and say that it symbolizes the future that management is striving to reach. Ask the group the following questions:

> If management wants employees to reach the goal, what would be a typical employee response?
>
> How should the Driving Forces act in order to change the organization?

5. Tell the Driving Forces to push the broomstick to attempt to reach the future, and remind the Restraining Forces that they are to resist any change.

6. As the Driving Forces push, the Restraining Forces typically push back to resist the change. When this starts to happen, stop the activity and ask what is happening. (*Answer:* When the Driving Forces push, the Restraining Forces push back harder to resist the change.) Tell participants that this is called the Boomerang Effect, a problem that is all too common in organizations as action creates an equal reaction.

7. Ask the group what can be done to lessen the Boomerang Effect. (*Answer:* Remove one person from the Restraining group.) Explain that removing a Restraining Force is only a first step. Remove one of the people from the Restraining Forces and then have the Driving Forces again attempt to push for change, symbolized by the line of tape. After a few minutes, stop the activity again.

8. At this point, the Driving Forces should have made some progress, but should not have reached the "future" yet. Note that there is still a lot of resistance to change and that it will continue as long as there are restraining forces. Suggest that there may be other possible ways to implement the change, and ask participants to brainstorm some ideas as you write them on the flip chart.

9. Facilitate the discussion, repeating, if necessary, that removing more Restraining Forces still leaves resistance in place, although weakened. When someone suggests that a Restraining Force must become a Driving Force, demonstrate with the volunteers. There will still be some resistance, but the Driving Forces will be considerably strengthened, allowing the group to reach the "future" state.

10. Give everyone copies of the *Broomstick Force Field Practice* and either have them practice individually or in small groups naming Driving and Restraining Forces. When everyone has finished, discuss the forces and post them on the flip chart.

11. Note on the flip chart:

Movement toward a future state is facilitated by removal or weakening of restraining forces and by the addition and strengthening of driving forces.

Discussion

At the end of the activity, have the volunteers describe the experience and give their reactions to it. Have them share what they have learned. Post their responses on the flip chart and also give everyone a copy of the *Broomstick Exercise: Creating a Force Field Analysis* sheet and the *Broomstick Debriefing* sheet to use in the future when facing change, whether welcome or not.

Discuss the concept of a Force Field Analysis and give participants an opportunity to describe an example within their own organization.

End by helping the participants see that learning to increase driving forces for change rather than simply removing resistance can be a positive and almost revolutionary experience. Encourage the participants to look for restraining forces in their organizations that can be removed or transformed into driving forces.

Source
M. K. Key, Blair Nickle, and Caroline Portis

Reference

Deming, W. E. (1986). *Out of the crisis.* Cambridge, MA: Massachusetts Institute of Technology, Center for Advanced Engineering Study.

Executive Learning, Inc., and Quorum Health Resources, Inc. (1993). *Creating the environment for continuous improvement,* unpublished course.

Lewin, K. (1951). *Field theory in social science.* New York: Harper & Row.

Broomstick Force Field Analysis Example

Desired State: A personal leadership style characterized by participation and collaboration.

Present State: A traditional leadership style characterized by authoritarian control.

Driving Forces	Restraining Forces
Changing work force →	← Past rewards for old style
Capability of workers →	← Fear of losing control
Top management direction →	← Workers' inexperience at decision making
Geographic dispersion of work force →	← Changing work force
Desire to be participative →	← Change is work!
Tired of making all decisions →	← Some worker resistance to taking responsibility
Need for more employee input/information →	← It there's a mistake, I am blamed
Increased span of control →	← Lack of time to focus on my skills and workers' skills

Present State   **Desired State**

Broomstick Force Field Practice

Desired State: A culture that works for continuous improvement and exemplifies Deming's fourteen points

Present State: A traditional, authoritarian organization

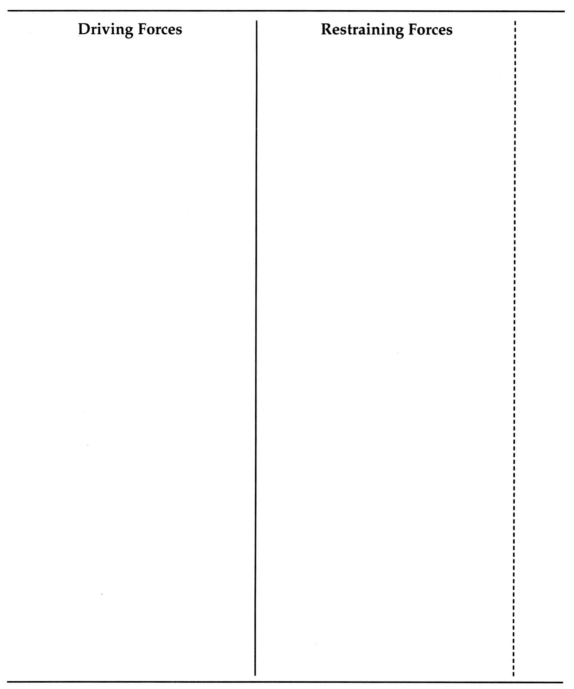

Driving Forces	Restraining Forces

Present State   Desired State

Broomstick Exercise: Creating a Force Field Analysis

Instructions: Use this sheet as a tool to display driving and restraining forces that increase or decrease the likelihood of successfully implementing any future organizational change.

1. Describe the *desired* organizational state.
2. Describe the *present* organizational state.
3. Construct the Force Field diagram:

   Draw two parallel vertical lines, a dashed line on the far right of the page, and a solid line down the center.

   Label the dashed line "desired state" and the solid line "present state" at the bottom of the page.

   On the left side of the solid line, list forces that will influence movement *toward* the desired state. Label these forces "Driving Forces" at the top of the page.

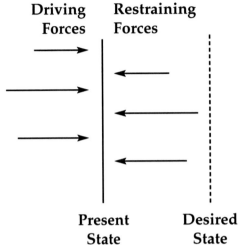

On the right side of the solid line, list forces that will *prevent* movement toward the desired state. Label these forces "Restraining Forces" at the top of the page.

Draw an arrow from each force toward the solid line, representing the magnitude of each force by varying the length of each arrow.

Broomstick Debriefing

When two sides polarize about a change, pushing for it and against it at the same time, the change will become difficult and unmanageable. Remember the following points from the Broomstick activity when facing future organizational change:

- When management wants to make a change, it typically increases the driving forces for the change. Often, this results in an increased push from restraining forces and the resulting Boomerang Effect.

- From the demonstration, it is clear that pushing back does not work. Working to remove some of the restraining forces is the first step for implementing change.

- Even when some restraining forces have been neutralized or removed, the driving forces probably still cannot push the remaining restraining forces into the future desired state.

- The logical step is to change the direction of the restraining forces. Turning a restraining force into a driving force—which adds strength to the driving forces and weakens the restraining forces at the same time—creates a more open pathway to the desired, future change state.

Creating Aim

Objective

- To create an "information organization" using purpose, vision, and values

Uses

This activity is for organizations without a clear sense of purpose or those that need to refocus. It serves as an introduction to concepts that can be taken back to the job site.

Time

Forty-five to sixty minutes

Audience

Any number, any level

Handouts, Materials, and Equipment

- A flip chart and markers
- Masking tape

Procedure

1. Tell participants that successful leaders are asked to carry out many difficult tasks. Planning for the future, managing organizational change, and coping with demanding employees and clients can fracture the nerves of even the most successful leaders. Say that although much is demanded of leaders in organizations today, effective leaders share one important attribute: They have recognized the importance of a clear sense of purpose, vision, and values to guide an organization toward success.

2. Ask participants to define "purpose," and write their answers on the flip chart, noting that a statement of organizational purpose must answer the question: "Why do we exist?" Tell people that the most effective statements are short and concise, with each word carrying significant meaning. Remind them that organizational purpose is based on customer needs, not on products produced.

3. Tape the definitions of purpose on the wall and then have participants define "vision." Again, record their comments on the flip chart. Most people will describe

vision as a means of focusing on an organization's future. After they have listed several possible definitions, say that vision describes an "ideal present," that is, what the present would look like if it were perfect. Mention that it is impossible to predict the future, so focusing on the ideal present in a vision statement allows individuals to focus both on the present and on the future. Say that a vision statement, much like a purpose statement, should be short and concise, allowing room for individuals to align their personal missions or purposes with it. Give them an example of a vision statement with an "ideal present," John F. Kennedy's desire to put "a man on the moon." It is short, concise, and paints a clear visual picture for all who share the vision. Tell them that the purpose in this case might be "to conquer space," which answers the question, "Why do we exist?" Post the definitions of vision on the wall.

4. Have the group define values and list some values that are important to them in their working environments. Write what they say on the flip chart and ask: "If you were starting an organization on Mars today, what values would you bring to Mars?" Note that an organization's purpose and vision should incorporate a variety of values from individuals in the organization. Post their list of values on the wall.

5. Discuss the value of organizational aim, a combination of purpose, vision, and values, using the following points and other points that are suggested by the participants. Write these and other suggestions on the flip chart using various marker colors. Examples include: provides clarity, provides focus, serves as a means of measuring progress, encourages collaboration and commitment, fosters organization unity, and allows organizational alignment.

6. Write and discuss the following steps for creating organizational aim in a hypothetical company:

Have each person reflect silently and then write down thoughts, ideas, or phrases relating to the organization's main purpose.

Have each person brainstorm ways to articulate the organization's ideal present.

Solicit one or more ideas from each person until everyone has contributed. Record all ideas on flip charts.

Discuss the ideas contributed by the group and make sure all participants fully understand the ideas presented.

Allow the group to continue the discussion until there is consensus on a draft of the vision statement.

Have group members discuss their values. How do their values align with the stated purpose and vision? If they do not align, ask them to adjust the purpose and vision statements.

7. Remind participants that most organizational statements of aim need constant revision and that statements of purpose, vision, and values should be reviewed by others. Tell them that it often is effective to let the statement sit for a few days before revising it.

8. Wrap up the session by reviewing all the points on the posted flip charts with participants and having them brainstorm some ways to take what they have learned back into their organizations.

Discussion

Explain to the participants that once an organizational aim has been finalized, it should be posted publicly in a place that is well trafficked. It also should be referred to in meetings when individuals are losing sight of their goals and directions. Tell them that it is extremely important that the statement be revised periodically to remain consistent with organizational and market changes.

Have the participants discuss their own organizational statements of purpose or aim, answering the following questions:

Why are the statements successful? What works and what does not?

How can they be improved?

Are they well articulated to employees?

Is the overall aim valued by employees as an integral component of the organization?

Variation

To provide practice, you can use the following activity the next day or after a break. Form groups of five and use the following steps to help participants develop a statement of organizational aim for a hypothetical company:

1. Tell participants: "You are an employee of Watch Your Step International that makes hiking gear for mountain climbers worldwide. Your sales last year were $400 million. Your products include insulated waterproof hiking boots, rain gear, and backpacks equipped with pouches for food, sleeping bags, and clothing. In addition, you make climbing ropes and stakes for steep inclines. You currently have 12,000 employees worldwide and you are expanding.

2. Assign the following executive roles in each group: Sales and Marketing Vice President, Director of Product Development, Financial Vice President, Production Manager, and Executive Director/CEO. Ask the CEO in each group to lead the discussion as they develop an organizational aim for the company.

3. After each group has developed an aim, have the groups share their statements with the others. Discuss their thoughts concerning this process.

Source
M. K. Key and Scott Fisher

Reference

Kouzes, J. M., & Posner, B. Z. (1990). *The leadership challenge: How to get things done in organizations.* San Francisco: Jossey-Bass.

Helping Others Deal with Change

Objectives
- To identify how leaders can help others deal with change
- To understand the stages of the change process

Uses
This activity is helpful for any group of managers or supervisors in an organization undergoing change.

Time
Thirty to sixty minutes, depending on number of participants

Audience
Any number, at any level with responsibility for change

Handouts, Materials, and Equipment
- Flip chart and markers
- One copy of *Helping Others Deal with Change Handout* for each participant
- One copy of the *Helping Others Deal with Change Scenarios* for each participant

Procedure
1. Tell participants that effective leaders are comfortable with change; in fact, they expect change to lead to opportunities that initiate *further change*. They learn from changes they made in the past and apply their experiences to future changes. Say that a good leader must be ready to help others embrace change in order to find innovative means of planning and implementing the change. Explain that the activity consists of a discussion of how leaders can help others overcome their natural resistance to change. Urge everyone to participate fully to gain the most benefit.

2. Ask participants to think back to a recent time when they observed others who were facing an unwanted change. Ask them to reflect on what those people did, for better or for worse. Ask whether there was resistance and for what possible reasons. List their answers on the flip chart.

3. Ask participants to recall a time when they had to make a change themselves. How did they introduce the change to their followers? Ask them to list what did and did not work during the introduction of the change while you list their comments on the flip chart under "worked" and "did not work."

4. Give each participant a copy of the *Helping Others Deal with Change Handout.* Give them time to read the handout and then lead a discussion, using examples from your own experience. First, describe a situation in which a leader neglected to follow all of the outlined steps and thus the followers' reactions were not positive. Then give an example of a smooth and effective change process in which all or most of the steps were followed.

5. Have participants share some of their own experiences in which using the steps has led to successful results.

6. Form small groups, distribute the *Helping Others Deal with Change Scenarios,* and tell the groups to discuss how they would help their followers deal with each scenario.

7. After fifteen minutes, solicit suggestions from the groups and list them on the flip chart.

Discussion

Discuss with the entire group how to use the ideas from the handouts and flip chart when leading others through a change.

Source
M. K. Key and Scott Fisher

Helping Others Deal with Change Handout

Instructions: Review the following steps for working with people and overcoming their resistance to change. Think of times when you have used these steps yourself or witnessed their use with others. Be prepared to share these experiences in some detail with the group and to suggest ways to use this list in the present change situation.

1. Set the stage for change by sharing personal experiences involving change.

2. Provide a history of the anticipated change and the present situation, give reasons for any changes, and outline the benefits of the change for the organization.

3. Help individuals to see the potential impact of the change by listing the skills and experiences they currently possess and the skills they will need to acquire in the future. Listen carefully to their questions and concerns.

4. Tell people what will *not* be changed.

5. List pros and cons associated with the change, identifying inhibiting forces against the change and positive forces for the change.

6. Agree what resources and strategies will be needed for change. List the necessary activities and decide on a timetable.

7. Celebrate by confirming the partnership for the change. Acknowledge and thank individuals for their cooperation.

Helping Others Deal with Change Scenarios

Instructions: Discuss how you would help your followers to deal with change in each of the following situations. Be as specific as possible. Be prepared to discuss your suggestions in the large group.

1. Your department must be downsized by 5 percent.

2. Your company plans to move from a manual to a computer invoicing system.

3. Your plant is changing from a team manufacturing process in which each employee does one part of the whole assembly process to an individual process in which each employee assembles an entire product.

4. Your top client has chosen to sign with a competitor and 25 percent of sales must be replaced.

5. Your company is moving from a supervisory management system to a team system.

Turning Misery into Merriment

Objectives

- To show that one's intent can change one's thinking
- To offer ways to handle change perceived as threatening
- To demonstrate the healing power of humor

Uses

The activity is intended to augment a discussion about chaotic change.

Audience

All levels of employees, especially people facing an upsetting change or living with the aftermath of one

Time

Twenty to thirty minutes

Handouts, Materials, and Equipment

- Pencils and paper for each participant
- A greeting card verse, a haiku poem, a limerick, a short humorous paragraph, or a pertinent cartoon

Procedure

1. Explain to the group that humor can be a healing force in times of stress and change.
2. Instruct participants to share with partners (or trios if necessary) a really upsetting change in their business or personal lives.
3. After each person has shared, have them work together with their partners to write something humorous about each traumatic change event. To illustrate, read an example of a humorous greeting card verse, haiku poem, limerick, or cartoon based on difficult changes.
4. After about ten minutes, call time and ask each pair to share its result.

Discussion

Ask the participants to discuss their reactions to the activity, using the following questions:

How did you feel as you recalled your past traumatic experience?

What effect did using humor have on your perceptions of your past experiences?

What can you generalize about ways to look at your current situation?

How can you use humor to help with future difficult situations?

Variation

Use as a follow-up for guiding groups through the serious steps of major change.

Source
Anne Durrum Robinson

Clarifying Expectations

Guaranteed to Fail

Objective

- To encourage the participants to take personal responsibility for instructional outcomes

Uses

This activity also can be used for team building, energizing, values clarification, creativity training, or implementation.

Audience

Participants at the beginning of any training workshop

Time

Fifteen to sixty minutes (see Variations)

Handouts, Materials, and Equipment

- One copy of *Guaranteed to Fail: Double-Reversal Technique* for each participant
- Paper and a pencil for each participant
- A 3″ × 5″ card for each participant
- A flip chart and markers
- A stopwatch or electronic timer
- A whistle

Procedure

1. Welcome the participants and tell them you are going to start with an individual brainstorming activity. Ask each participant to take a sheet of paper and write down several ideas in response to the following question:

   What can I do to ensure that this workshop is absolutely useless for me?

2. Repeat the question and write it on the flip chart to focus the participants' attention on this strange task. Announce a two-minute time limit and tell them to begin.

3. Wait while the participants write down their responses, then give some additional prompts. After about a minute, blow the whistle to get their attention. Ask the following probing questions and write them on the flip chart:

What types of personal thoughts would reduce the value of the workshop for you?

What can you tell yourself to ensure the failure of the workshop?

How could you interact with the other participants to ensure that the workshop becomes completely useless?

How could you interact with the facilitator to ensure that you gain nothing from the workshop?

4. Pause for about a minute while the participants add items to their lists, then blow the whistle, and ask them to stop writing. Invite them to call out ideas that are most likely to guarantee a totally worthless workshop. Write these on the flip chart. Stop when there are ten items.

5. Explain that, of course, your actual goal for the workshop is the opposite. You want to ensure that everyone obtains the most value from the workshop and you plan to do your best to achieve this goal. Say that you need help from them. Now that they have figured out ingenious ways to avoid learning anything, ask them to convert their ideas into positive suggestions.

6. Use the first item on the flip chart as an example and turn it around 180 degrees. Ask the participants to help you convert the other items into positive suggestions, pointing out that some items may be converted into more than one positive suggestion. Write their suggestions on the flip chart.

7. Ask the participants to write personal contracts for learning on their papers. When they have finished, ask them to identify their top three guidelines for extracting the maximum value from the workshop.

8. While they are doing this, hand out 3″ × 5″ cards to each person. Ask them to fold the cards in half horizontally like a tent and to write their three guidelines for obtaining value from the workshop on the side of the "tent" facing them to provide a reminder throughout the session.

Discussion

Debrief the activity by giving each participant a copy of the *Guaranteed to Fail: Double-Reversal Technique.* Explain that most people find it easier to come up with negative, destructive strategies than positive, constructive ones. Being asked to develop strategies for failure is so unusual that most people become very creative and unconventional in thinking of both negative and positive.

Variations

1. If there is not enough time for participants to write their responses, ask them to call out responses and then paraphrase them on the flip chart and ask for ways to reverse them, rather than having people create personal contracts.

2. If there is ample time, another activity can be used right away to reinforce the concept of double reversal for solving a common problem.

3. If not used at the beginning of a session, this activity can be used immediately after a lunch break to combat the post-lunch blahs, substituting the question: "How can we become drowsy and passive?"

4. The activity can be used near the end of a workshop to assist transfer to the workplace by asking: "How can we ensure that none of the new skills and concepts we have learned will ever be used?"

Source
Sivasailam "Thiagi" Thiagarajan and Raja Thiagarajan

Guaranteed to Fail: Double-Reversal Technique

Instructions:

1. Write down one or more goals related to a problem or to an opportunity. Be sure that each goal statement contains a verb and an object (for example, "motivate employees"). Select one of the goals for further exploration.

2. Write the "laog" (pronounced lay-augh) or exact opposite of each goal by replacing the verb in each goal with its antonym. For example, if the goal is to motivate employees, the laog is to demotivate or discourage employees.

3. Brainstorm and write down strategies for achieving the laog, ignoring the actual goal. For example: *How to demotivate employees:*

    Increase employee work load.

    Prevent employees from working on projects they enjoy.

    Make sure that employee assignments are dull, boring, and mechanical.

    Withhold feedback from employees.

    Threaten to fire employees.

    Reduce employees' salaries.

    Be unpredictable.

4. Now reverse strategies by writing the opposite of each strategy for achieving the laog. For example: *Withhold information from employees.*

    Reversal: Share all critical information with employees.

5. Try to reverse all the strategies on the list. However, if any strategy appears to be irrelevant, ignore it. Some strategies may be reversed in more than one way. For example: *Punish employees in public.*

    Reversal 1: Praise employees in public.

    Reversal 2: Punish employees privately.

    Reversal 3: Do not punish employees.

6. Edit the list of reverse strategies. They then become strategies for achieving the original goal. Examine each reverse strategy and rewrite it to ensure its applicability for achieving the goal.

7. Expand the list as much as possible as the edited list of reverse strategies may suggest additional ideas.

8. Repeat the process with other goal statements. Select another goal statement, state its laog, write strategies for achieving this laog, and list the reverse strategies.

The Tie That Binds

Objectives
- To clarify workshop goals and objectives
- To reach agreement about workshop goals and objectives

Uses
This activity is useful for new groups or for groups that seem uncertain about workshop objectives. It is also a good introduction to intergroup team building and can be used as an icebreaker or energizer.

Audience
Two, four, or six groups of three or four participants each

Time
Fifteen to twenty minutes

Handouts, Materials, and Equipment
- One four-foot length of lightweight rope or heavy twine for each group
- Paper and pencils for each group

Procedure
1. Form participants into two, four, or six groups of three or four each and distribute a length of rope and paper and pencils to each group.
2. Have each group generate a list of at least three expectations they have in common for the workshop and write them down.
3. Tell the groups to tie a knot in the rope to represent each expectation they have agreed on. Explain that knots should be spaced approximately one foot apart, beginning about one foot from the end. After three expectations have been agreed on, there should be three knots in the middle of the rope.
4. When all groups have finished, ask each group in turn to share its expectations with the large group, holding up each knot as they discuss the expectation it represents.

5. Now ask groups to pair up with another group and to identify common expectations. They should tie their ropes together as soon as they agree that their expectations are mutual. If agreement cannot be achieved easily, additional knots may be tied in either rope, representing additional expectations one group may hold that the other does not.

6. If there are two groups, and they agree on expectations, they may tie both ends of their ropes together to form a circle. If there are four or six groups, each pair of groups is to work toward agreeing on mutual expectations in order to tie its ropes together until all the ropes are connected. (*Note:* Regardless of the number of groups, the final product should be one large, knotted rope tied together in a big loop, representing expectations with which all participants can agree.)

7. After all the ropes are tied together, ask participants to hold the rope in front of them as they stand in a circle facing one another. Ask if there are any remaining expectations that everyone can agree to. If so, have them untie the rope at any point and add a new knot to represent the new expectation.

8. Instruct the participants to pull gently outward on the rope simultaneously. Then ask people on one side of the rope circle to pull gently toward themselves while those on the other side allow themselves to be pulled toward the center of the circle. (Emphasize the word "gently.")

Discussion

Discuss with participants what the activity illustrates about expectations and teamwork. They should see that expectations of all group members must be brought out and clarified before a group can "pull together." The same is true about one group working with another and for multiple groups working together. Explain that linking the ropes is symbolic of how individuals within groups must link with one another and how groups must link with one another to achieve group and organizational objectives. Help them to see that when everyone pulled equally on the rope, the circle maintained its integrity, but when only some people pulled, the circle was lost. Ask what this means for everyone in the workshop or team-building event.

Source
Arthur VanGundy

We've Got Rhythm

Objectives

- To help participants develop mutual understanding of a workshop's goals
- To create an environment conducive to group work

Uses

This activity is also useful at the beginning of training sessions as a get-acquainted activity or for a team-building or climate-setting workshop.

Audience

All levels in small- to medium-sized groups

Time

Approximately ten minutes

Handouts, Materials, and Equipment

- Pencils without erasers for each participant
- Any hard object capable of making a sound when struck by a pencil, such as a table, metal chair, or clipboard
- A flip chart and markers

Procedure

1. Instruct participants to sit in a circle with a table or chair in the middle and give each person one pencil.
2. Ask each person, in turn, to use the pencil to drum out his or her name in syncopated rhythm while simultaneously saying it. (For example, the name "Mary Tyler Moore" could be said with equal emphasis on each syllable: Mar-y Ty-ler Moore. Or with accent only on the first syllables: *Mar'*-y *Ty'*-ler *Moore'*. Or, the second syllable: Mar-*y'* Ty-*ler'* Moore. Or with alternate accented syllables: *Mar'*-y Ty-*ler'* *Moore'*.
3. Tell participants to write down three short statements about what they expect to learn from the workshop (e.g., Learn how to listen better.).

4. Have each participant select one of his or her expectations and play it in syncopated rhythm while saying it out loud, as each did with his or her name. Repeat until all participants have played and spoken their expectations while you record them on the flip chart.

5. Point to each statement and ask for volunteers, other than the person who contributed it, to explain what it means. If necessary, ask the person who contributed it to clarify.

Discussion

Lead a discussion of all the statements and develop a consensus as to the group's expectations of the session, comparing their expectations with yours and adjusting as needed. Ask the group questions such as:

How did the different rhythms affect your understanding of the expectations people had?

Did you understand and retain the statements more easily than if they had just been spoken? If so, why?

Variations

1. Substitute actual rhythm instruments such as unpitched rhythm instruments and a bass drum or a drum machine connected to an amplifier.

2. Have participants present their other two statements in round-robin fashion.

Source
Janice Kilgore and Arthur VanGundy

Wall Murals

Objectives

- To provide a fun, creative way to clarify training expectations
- To help participants develop consensus about session objectives

Uses

This activity is intended for getting acquainted or warming up a group at the start of a training session.

Audience

All levels in groups of four to ten

Time

Fifteen to twenty minutes

Handouts, Materials, and Equipment

- Enough butcher paper or flip-chart paper to cover one wall at least eight feet long
- Markers for each participant
- A supply of colored stickers such as dots, stars, rectangles, and Post-it® Notes for each participant
- Several lengths of colored yarn or string
- Several rolls each of masking and cellophane tape
- Magazines that contain pictures, at least one for every two participants
- Several pairs of scissors
- A flip chart and markers

Procedure

1. Attach the butcher paper or flip-chart sheets on one wall of the room prior to the session and place all the other materials on a table where they are available to the participants.

2. Explain that the purpose of this activity is to clarify expectations about the training event. Tell them that they will be creating collages to symbolize what they expect to obtain from the session.

3. Give as an example that someone might place adhesive dots in a circle and connect the dots using the yarn to indicate an expectation of shared communication and consensus decision making. Have the participants think for a few minutes about their expectations and then individually select whatever items they wish from the table and begin.

4. After everyone has finished his or her creation, have each person describe it to the large group.

5. Ask the group to review all of the creations and summarize group expectations on a flip chart and post it for the actual session.

Discussion

Check with participants to see whether creating an expression of their expectations helped to clarify them. Ask questions such as:

What worked well? What did not work well?

What was most surprising for you about doing this activity?

What did you learn about others' expectations?

Do you have other expectations that you were not able to express on your collage? What are they?

Are you better able to begin the session now than you were at the beginning?

Source
Arthur VanGundy

Climate Setting

Bond and Connect

Objective

- To help participants meet people in large groups or crowds

Uses

This activity was developed to help people who do not know one another very well become better acquainted when they need to work together or cooperate on projects. It also can be used as a climate-setting or communication activity.

Audience

Any

Time

Ten to twenty minutes

Handouts, Materials, and Equipment

- *Optional:* Old tennis balls, foam balls, or wadded paper

Procedure

1. Introduce the activity as a way to begin to meet as many people in the group as possible.
2. Lead participants through one or more of the following activities:

   Stand up, introduce yourself, and shake hands with people around you.

   Stand up, shift three people to the right, introduce yourself, and shake hands with people around you.

   Form groups of four or five while standing and share personal information for ninety seconds each about home towns, nicknames, hobbies, a creative thing you have done, one creative thing you would like to do, or one strange gift you have received or given.

   Group participants by state or region and give them three to five minutes to meet some other members of their groups.

Have the group create a "wave."

Form circles of eight to ten. Use old tennis balls, foam balls, or wadded paper and challenge participants to throw the objects around the group in alphabetical order according to first name. Time the groups to see how fast they can do this. (*Note:* This is a great communication and bonding activity that can be done in about ten minutes.)

Have participants form rows and then arrange themselves in alphabetical order without leaving their rows, either silently or by talking.

Have the entire group line up in alphabetical order.

Form a line according to years in the organization or years in attendance at the conference or other quantifiable data.

Discussion

Ask the group to share general reactions after each activity, especially if and how the activity contributed to bonding as a group. Talk about the type of climate the activity creates. For instance, a "wave" might create one type of climate, whereas lining up alphabetically might create another. Try to find reasons why this is true.

Source
Robert Alan Black

Feather Talk

Objectives

- To encourage open communication
- To test group consensus
- To introduce color and playfulness

Uses

This activity is used at the beginning of a session to encourage participant feedback and to establish a norm of open expression of both positive and negative feelings that often remain unstated because participants try to be polite. It can also be used for training in negotiation or communication.

Audience

All levels and types of people

Time

Twenty to thirty minutes

Handouts, Materials, and Equipment

- Red and green feathers, approximately twelve inches long, one of each color for each participant
- *Optional:* Colored index cards can be used in place of feathers, for a similar but less powerful impact

Procedure

1. Distribute one green feather and one red feather to each participant before the session begins.
2. After everyone is seated, explain that the red feather is to be held up to indicate *disagreement* with something you or another participant has just said; the green feather is to be used to express *agreement* or interject an example related to a previous comment.

3. Each time a red feather is raised during the workshop, stop to discuss the issue briefly. The more important the issue, the more time should be given to the discussion. Instruct them to see disagreement simply as additional data and as an opportunity to learn from one another. Do not allow participants to become defensive or argue for their positions.

Discussion

At the end of the session, discuss participant reactions to using the feathers, using questions such as these:

Were green feathers easier to use than the red feathers?

Was it easier to indicate your disagreement with a red feather than it was to speak up immediately? Why is that?

Why is it difficult to express negative comments?

What other ways can you think of to use the feathers during a workshop?

Variation

The facilitator can ask for a "show of feathers" to test the extent of disagreement or agreement on an issue, using the green feathers to represent "yes" or "I agree" and the red for "no" or "I disagree." Yellow feathers can be used to indicate "neutral" or "not sure."

Source
Deanna Berg

Perceptions

Objective
- To demonstrate how our perceptions shape how we feel about things

Uses
The activity can be used to train participants in general or creative thinking, as an icebreaker, or for team building.

Audience
Intact work teams with five to seven members each

Time
Ten to fifteen minutes

Handouts, Materials, and Equipment
- One sheet of paper for each participant
- A pen or pencil for each participant

Procedure
1. Have people divide up into their usual work teams and tell the groups you are going to give a test. Hand out paper and pens or pencils to each participant.
2. Read the following questions aloud, allowing everyone time to write down their answers:

   What is your name?

   What is your job?

   What do you like about your job?

   What is your definition of "work"?

   Are you creative?

   What animal (other than human) best reflects what you are like?

   What words can you associate with personal creativity on the job?

3. Have people discuss their answers in their groups, looking for patterns and ways to help one another be more creative on the job. After fifteen or twenty minutes, pull all groups together for a general discussion.

Discussion

To help guide a discussion of this activity, consider using the following questions to bring out ways to enhance personal and organizational creativity:

What are some ways to learn to like your job, to make it more interesting?

What were some of the definitions people had for "work"?

Were there other motivators than making money?

In what ways were people creative? How did they use their creativity on the job? How can you learn to do so?

How were the animals you chose reflective of you? Of your level of creativity?

What words came to mind to describe creativity in your organization? (If the answers are words such as "unused," "ignored," or "unwanted," creativity is obviously not fostered in the organization nor by the people themselves. Look for words such as "starlight," "moonbeams," or "flowers.")

Source
Roger J. Syverson

Rumperstickers

Objectives
- To provide a different type of introductory activity
- To encourage humor and creative levity

Uses
This activity is very useful to engage workshop participants quickly in a fun way.

Audience
All levels in small- to medium-sized groups

Time
Fifteen to thirty minutes

Handouts, Materials, and Equipment
- One rectangular strip of heavyweight card stock (approximately 3″ × 11″) for each participant. Each strip should have a hole punched at each end and a length of string approximately 24 inches long tied from one hole to the other.
- One black marker for each participant

Procedure
1. Hand out the strips of card stock and markers and ask participants to write humorous "rumperstickers." Make it clear that all messages should be in good taste.
2. When they have finished, instruct them to tie the rumperstickers around their rear ends and walk around reading one another's creations.
3. *Optional:* If desired, the participants can vote on the best message and award a prize.

Discussion

Ask the participants to discuss how well the activity worked to liven up the group and establish a humorous, positive climate. Also bring out any negative aspects and suggestions for improvement.

Variation

The activity can be used as a follow-up for guiding groups through the serious steps of major change.

Source
Anne Durrum Robinson

Vanity Plates

Objectives

- To warm up the participants and start their creative juices flowing
- To demonstrate the creativity that exists in the group
- To begin learning about one another

Uses

This activity provides a nonthreatening way to warm up participants using minimal materials.

Audience

Small groups at all levels

Time

Fifteen to thirty minutes

Handouts, Materials, and Equipment

- Paper and pencils for each participant
- A flip chart and markers
- Masking tape

Procedure

1. Tell participants that they will be using their creative talents during this activity. Tell them that research has shown that one characteristic of high intelligence and high creativity is the ability to make new connections among existing ideas. Say that learning to make new and more abstract connections will enrich and reinforce their learning of new material.

2. Ask participants to form small groups of three or four and assign them the task of creating one vanity plate per participant that illustrates that participant's special creative talents. Ask them to turn their paper horizontally and draw their plates as they would appear in whichever state or province they are from.

3. Write the following examples on the flip chart to help people start:

   IMCRE8V (I Am Creative)

   INOV8 (Innovate)

   TMSWRK (Teams Work)

   PROSPKR (Professional Speaker)

   CRE8VTHKG (Creative Thinking)

4. Answer any questions that come up while the groups are working. Stress that you want their vanity plates to be unique and to communicate the message well.

5. Have participants post their plates on the wall and allow people time to look at the others before calling people together for a closing discussion.

Discussion

In wrapping up, point out that creating headlines, diagrams, symbols, or license plates with eight or fewer letters and numbers means that they must condense their thoughts well so that others can understand the message. Discuss any difficulties they may have had in creating a vanity plate or in understanding someone else's plate.

Variation

Famous people or specific occupations rather than participant characteristics can be used to practice being creative.

Source
Robert Alan Black

Communication

Do You Hear What I Play?

Objectives

- To improve listening skills
- To improve communication

Uses

This activity assists in improving both the listening and telling skills involved in good communication.

Audience

All levels, individually or in small groups

Time

Thirty minutes

Handouts, Materials, and Equipment

- One small toy drum and drumsticks for each participant

Procedure

1. Introduce the objectives of the activity and give each person a drum.
2. Have participants divide up into pairs and move as far from others as possible so they are not distracted by the noise from other pairs.
3. Tell participants that one member of each pair should beat out a simple rhythm on the drum and then the other person must repeat the rhythm he or she has heard.
4. Then the first drummer is to slowly increase the complexity of the rhythms; have the second person repeat it correctly, and move on to a new pattern. Do this until the rhythms are too complex for the second person to repeat and then switch drummers and start over.

Discussion

Bring the group together to discuss the experience, asking questions such as:

What did you discover about yourself by doing this activity?

What conclusions, if any, can be drawn about how you communicate information to others?

What conclusions, if any, can be drawn about how effectively you listen as others communicate with you?

What implications can be drawn about resolving conflict?

What implications can be drawn about ways to increase your understanding of what others are saying?

Source
Suzanne E. Jonas

Incredible Difficulty of Communicating Simple Ideas

Objectives

- To demonstrate the difficulty of transmitting verbal descriptions accurately and reliably
- To show how important precision is for giving instructions and relaying information
- To learn how to understand the working assumptions of others when translating ideas from one person to another

Uses

The activity is helpful when problems have occurred from information being transferred inaccurately, when the situation calls for cooperation, or whenever miscommunications occur.

Audience

Any

Time

Thirty minutes

Handouts, Materials, and Equipment

- Two sheets of paper and a pencil for each participant

Procedure

1. Tell participants that the activity concerns miscommunication and instruct them to form pairs.

2. Hand out two sheets of paper and a pencil to each person; then ask each participant to draw a "picture" that contains three geometric shapes of any kind, size, or configuration, such as a circle, square, triangle, line, or point, *without allowing anyone else to see it.*

3. When everyone has finished, tell them that one member of each pair is to verbally describe his or her "picture" to the other person, who is to try to duplicate the image on his or her blank paper using the verbal description only.

4. When everyone has finished, have the other member of each pair describe his or her picture while the other person draws it.

5. Ask pairs to compare their results to see how close each came to the original and to note any differences for the large group discussion to follow.

Discussion

Lead a discussion of this activity as a graphic demonstration of the difficulties involved in communicating even simple, straightforward images and information to another person. Point out that the responsibility is often placed on the sender to understand the past experiences, thinking style, and aptitudes of the receiver, who must only be attentive. Guide the discussion with the following questions:

What techniques did you use during the activity that helped or hindered the receiver's understanding?

Were any errors encoded in the transmission?

Was any information distorted or misread by the receiver?

What additional cues could have helped the receiver to duplicate the drawing?

Are there similarities between relating a drawing and relating an idea? If so, what are they?

What does the sender need to know about the receiver to ensure a better communication?

What happens during the original encoding of the information, the transmission process, or the decoding process to produce a bad copy of a drawing or a total misunderstanding of an original idea?

What contributes to successful sending and receiving of information?

Source
Margaret J. King

Influence, Not Authority

Objective

- To develop awareness that context is as important as content when attempting to persuade

Uses

The activity provides practice in making persuasive presentations and allows participants to analyze, in depth, the factors that determine successful influencing.

Audience

Any in groups of four or five

Time

About twenty-five minutes for twenty participants; shorter or longer, depending on number

Handouts, Materials, and Equipment

- Four copies of *Persuasion Pointers* for each participant (more if there are more than four subgroups)
- A flip chart and markers

Procedure

1. Introduce the activity by saying:

   Ken Blanchard, author of The One-Minute Manager, *defines the key to successful leadership as "influence, not authority." Often, we do not realize the communication sins we are committing—sins that negate our influence and diminish our authority.*

2. Give each participant four copies of the Persuasion Pointers handout and read through it with everyone, remarking that the list of persuasion points on the handout will assist them—no matter what the circumstances—to put ideas across more clearly, to prime an audience for being receptive, and to structure presentations more logically and forcefully. Give them time to write notes on their copies.

3. Now ask for a volunteer to stand at the front with you for a minute. Explain that the person is playing Sue, your supervisor, and that they are to try to spot mistakes you make when you try to catch Sue's attention. Play your role by saying:

"Hi, Sue. Do you have a minute? I have a great idea I'd like to tell you about."

4. Allow the volunteer to be seated and then ask participants what you did wrong. They should have noticed the following:

> You have caught your supervisor "on the fly." It is much better to set up an appointment so that your idea can be given the attention it deserves.

> If you ask for a few minutes, that may be exactly what you receive.

> You should have been more specific, mentioning "A great idea for obtaining customer feedback," or whatever you had in mind.

5. Guide the group in generating a list of ten topics for discussion as you write them on the flip chart.

6. Divide the class into four groups of four to six members each. Allow ten minutes for each group to select a topic from the list and plan a persuasive five-minute presentation. Instruct them to select a spokesperson to deliver the presentation to the other groups.

7. Have groups take turns making presentations while the other participants use the handout to evaluate the presentation, checking all the items that apply.

8. Then ask each small group to meet for five or ten minutes to discuss and combine what they have said individually about the presentation onto one sheet.

9. Follow the same process until each small group's presentation has been evaluated by the other groups. Collect the sheets and give them to the groups that made the presentations.

10. Give each group an opportunity to discuss the feedback, while you circulate to make comments and suggestions.

Discussion

Lead a closing discussion using the following questions as guides:

> What did you see or hear that you especially liked?

> What did you find to be the least effective *technique* that was used?

> What place does humor have in persuasion?

> What is the connection between leadership and persuasion?

> What examples of outstanding persuasive skills can you think of? (One example is when President Kennedy persuaded many Americans to sacrifice comfort and security to join the Peace Corps.)

Variations

1. Use lighthearted topics such as: "Should we keep the same seats all day?" or "Should we finish early on Friday?"

2. Use the activity as a mid-session stimulator, using topics that reflect the content of the training.

3. Use the activity to summarize the day's events, using topics such as: "What is one thing we can do to transfer what we have learned back to our work site?"

Source
Marlene Caroselli

Persuasion Pointers

Name of presenter: _____

Topic: _____

Things to Do:

- Exhibit confidence.
- Be specific. Say "I have a plan to reduce costs" rather than "I have a great idea."
- Use visuals when appropriate.
- Do some homework.
- Listen to feedback.
- Cite successful precedents.
- Make an appointment in advance when presenting a proposal to a supervisor or other management personnel.
- Align the proposal with organizational thrusts (e.g., quality, reengineering, etc.).
- Cite benefits or "What's in It for Me?" (WIFM).
- Anticipate objections or questions and have answers ready.
- Suggest a trial period if rejection is likely.
- Make a plan in writing.
- Mention, if it is true, that the idea has already gained informal acceptance.
- Acknowledge possible pitfalls.
- Pause periodically and ask if the other person has questions.
- Provide a time line.
- Have benchmarking data available, if possible.
- Cite an authority who endorses the idea.
- Discuss expected outcomes.
- Relate the proposal, directly or indirectly, to customer satisfaction.
- Be realistic.
- Have alternative suggestions ready.
- Thank the listener for his or her time.
- Conclude by mentioning next steps.

Comments:

Persuasion Pointers (continued)

Things Not to Do:

- Interrupt while the other person is talking.
- Mention cost or other negative details prior to making the "pitch."
- Set up for a "yes-or-no" response. Offer options as appropriate.
- Apologize.
- Push for an immediate answer.
- Limit the time allotted by asking, "Do you have a few minutes?"
- Be offended by rejection. Ask, "What can I do to make the proposal more viable?"
- Meet at a time when the other person is not likely to be receptive.
- Become sidetracked.
- Be afraid to state your faith in the idea.
- Validate the need for something by blaming others for the problem.
- Dance around the topic.
- Show doubt about the worth of the idea.
- Neglect to ask for feedback.
- Overwhelm the listener by describing how extensively he or she would be involved.
- Permit the scope of the proposal to go far beyond the comfort level of the listener.
- Forget to have paper and pen ready to take notes.
- Abandon the project entirely if it is not favorably received. Ask which pieces could be salvaged.
- Avoid eye contact.
- Mumble.
- Become defensive.
- Overlook safety, legal, or union issues related to the plan.
- Be thrown by tough questions.
- Forget to use the pronoun "we" as often as you use "I."

Comments:

It's Crystal Clear to Me

Objectives

- To demonstrate that communication is an art, not a science
- To increase group awareness of the importance of clear communication

Uses

The activity can be used prior to day-long or longer meetings to facilitate more effective and productive communication.

Audience

Any level, in groups of twenty or fewer

Time

About twenty minutes

Handouts, Materials, and Equipment

- Crystals, one per person (available from a museum or educational store)
- A quote about communication that is short enough to remember, yet somewhat complex, such as "True communication is a creation that has the power to shape, determine, and alter the course and quality of our lives."
- A flip chart and markers

Procedure

1. Form the group into a rough circle, either standing or seated.
2. Whisper the quote you have chosen to one member of the group. Say it only once! Ask each person to pass the quote to the next person in the circle as accurately as possible. Ask the last person who receives it to repeat the quote aloud to the group. Write it on the flip chart, along with the original quote.

Discussion

Discuss the outcome by saying that actual communication is often just as muddled. Ask the participants if they can recall times when they might have misunderstood something or needed clarification of something that was said and did not or could not ask for it. Discuss their answers and possible reasons for their hesitation to ask questions.

Hand out the crystals, one per person. Ask that for the rest of the meeting, people ask for clarification by holding up their crystals whenever they would like or need further crystallization of a sentence, word, or expression. Gain their commitment to remind one another of the obligation to communicate well with others and to ask clarifying questions.

Source
Leslie Berger and Nance Guilmartin

Language Bias

Objectives

- To identify common biases in language
- To find appropriate substitutions for biased language
- To explore language differences in formal and informal communication settings

Uses

The activity is helpful during general employee training, especially for diversity training.

Time

Fifteen to thirty minutes

Handouts, Materials, and Equipment

- A copy of the *Language Bias Handout Trainer's Notes* for the facilitator
- One copy of the *Language Bias Handout* for each participant
- Pencils or highlighters for participants
- A flip chart or whiteboard and markers

Procedure

1. Give out the *Language Bias Handout* and read it aloud as participants follow along. Try to read without emphasis on any particular words or phrases.

2. Ask the participants to identify (individually) biased language they hear as you read and to mark it so that they can find it later.

3. When you have finished reading, ask them to choose bias-free substitutes for the words or phrases they have identified as biased and to write them on their handouts. Tell them that their replacements cannot change the meaning of the passage.

4. When everyone has finished, have people volunteer their words and their replacements while you write them on the flip chart or whiteboard.

Discussion

Use the following questions to guide a discussion of the activity:

Were you able to identify all the examples of biased language? If not, why do you think that you did not?

Does language shape the way we view others? How?

Do you think that "politically correct" language is necessary in formal communication settings such as an office? Why or why not?

How does our language differ in formal and informal settings?

Should the context and setting of a conversation play a role in choosing appropriate language? Why or why not?

How might our relationship with a communication partner or group help shape our language choices? Do we tailor our language to the particular relationship? Should we?

What did you learn about your own use of language?

Do you avoid language bias in your everyday speech? If not, what can you do to change?

Did you originally envision an all-male fire crew? How do biases like these shape our everyday perceptions?

Source
Melinda M. Morris

Language Bias Handout Trainer's Notes

- Paul is not Chinese; he is a Chinese-American because he was born in California.
- Katie is a twenty-four-year-old woman.
- The "old geezer" is an older adult or senior citizen.
- Deaf people are hearing impaired.
- A butch-sounding girl might be a woman with a deep voice.
- Mankind might be humankind or all people.
- Women are brave, too.

Language Bias Handout

Directions: As I read the following passage, find examples of biased language and mark them on your copy. When I have finished, you will be given an opportunity to find bias-free replacements for the words you have identified, but you are not to change the overall meaning of the passage.

Paul is a Chinese fireman who was born in California. One day, he received a call about a fire at the house of a twenty-four-year-old girl named Katie. When Paul and his fire crew arrived at the address they were given, he saw an old geezer sitting on the porch. "Where is the fire?" asked Paul. The old geezer was so deaf that she did not hear Paul's question. At that moment, Paul heard a butch-sounding girl yell at him: "Hey, the fire is over here!"

He quickly drove his fire truck to the next street, where he saw a burning house. Paul turned on his fire hose to fight the fire. He knew that he had to hurry and bring the situation under control because he was the only man there. Finally, the fire was extinguished. All of mankind should be grateful for brave men like Paul.

Creativity

Belt It Out

Objectives

- To demonstrate the need to view problems from different perspectives
- To practice fluent idea generation

Uses

The activity is useful to train participants in the creative-thinking process.

Audience

Any

Time

Five to ten minutes

Handouts, Materials, and Equipment

- An overhead projector and transparencies or a flip chart and markers
- Paper and pens or pencils for participants

Procedure

1. Write the word "BELT" in large letters on a transparency or flip-chart pad.

2. Hand out paper and pencils and ask the participants to generate all the different uses they can think of for an unlimited supply of belts and to write them down *without sharing with anyone else.* Encourage them to really stretch their thinking.

3. After participants seem to be running out of ideas, ask whether they have considered different types of "belts," such as the Bible Belt, going on a drinking belt, the magnetic belt, a highway belt, a fan belt, or a tool belt. Give them more time to write down their ideas and have people share one or two of their more creative items.

Discussion

Lead a discussion of why their thinking was limited to belts worn with clothing (which it typically will be) and why, when you asked them to stretch their thinking a little they probably came up with creative uses for a belt, but may not have thought of other types of belt. If some members of the group did expand the definition of a belt, ask them to describe their thinking processes to the group.

Source
Roger J. Syverson

It Just Doesn't Add Up

Objectives

- To demonstrate how easy it is to become trapped in thinking ruts
- To become aware of how our security needs block our thinking

Uses

This activity helps jolt people out of complacent thinking. It is especially useful for people who do not think they need help with creative thinking.

Audience

All levels, any size group

Time

Fifteen minutes

Handouts, Materials, and Equipment

- A transparency of the *It Just Doesn't Add Up Problem*
- An overhead projector
- A sheet of cardboard or piece of paper to cover the transparency

Procedure

1. Prior to the session, make a transparency of the *It Just Doesn't Add Up Problem*.
2. Tell participants that you are going to ask them to add up cumulative totals for a column of whole, round numbers. Give them an example, saying that if the first number were ten and the second fifteen, they would say, "twenty-five," and if the next number were five, they would say, "thirty." Ask if there are any questions and repeat the example if necessary.
3. Before displaying the problem on an overhead projector, cover up all except the first number ("1,000") with a piece of paper or cardboard. Tell the participants they are to add up the numbers cumulatively and to do so aloud and simultaneously.

4. Tell them to start with the first number they see. After they have said "one thousand," reveal the next number ("40") and encourage them to add it to 1,000 and give the answer out loud (if they have not already done so). They now should be able to continue without any additional prompting.

5. Continue revealing one number at a time, pausing slightly before revealing the last number ("10"). Do not reveal the answer yet. When the audience starts to say an answer, there usually is some hesitation and then a blurting out of "five thousand." If you hesitate just a moment before revealing the answer ("4,100") you may even hear a few people say "six thousand." The gasps will begin as soon as everyone sees the correct answer.

6. Only a small percentage of people will have called out the correct answer. Ask the group to discuss why this is true. (*One answer:* Because you create a pattern involving thousands: 1,000, 2,000, 3,000, 4,000, 5,000, just as if you were adding the numbers 1 through 5. This simple process creates an unjustified confidence in what the next response will be. And then, watch out! Right at the end, our brains go into overdrive trying to figure out the correct response. Even though the mouth says five thousand, the brain seems to know that this is not right, but it is not quite sure what is.)

Discussion

Note that most people could total the numbers correctly if they were presented with all of the data at once. Instead, you forced them into a patterned response that was difficult to break. Ask why this happened and if it is possible to add the numbers correctly using this method. Note that we often succumb to our security needs or conditioning and stay with the same old way of responding. Ask the participants to discuss other examples of this behavior in their lives.

Have the participants discuss how often we fail to solve problems when they are defined by someone else or when we use someone else's assumptions about how to solve them. Discuss which situation is dealt with more easily.

Source
Unknown

$$
\begin{array}{r}
1,000 \\
40 \\
1,000 \\
30 \\
1,000 \\
20 \\
1,000 \\
10 \\
\hline
4,100
\end{array}
$$

More Ideas Than You!

Objectives

- To learn about brainstorming and brainwriting
- To compare the effectiveness of brainstorming and brainwriting

Uses

The activity is good for idea generation training and for teaching brainstorming techniques.

Audience

Any, with a minimum of two groups of three to five each

Time

Fifteen minutes

Handouts, Materials, and Equipment

- Paper and a pencil for each participant
- One deck of index cards for each group
- One copy of the *More Ideas Than You! Brainstorming Instructions* for each participant
- One copy of the *More Ideas Than You! Brainwriting Instructions* for each participant

Procedure

1. Explain the objectives of the activity, noting that most people are not aware that there is an alternative to traditional brainstorming known as "brainwriting." Define brainwriting as the silent, written generation of ideas in a group.

2. Distribute the *More Ideas Than You! Brainstorming Instructions* to each participant. Have the participants follow along while you read the instructions aloud. Answer any questions. Then do the same for the brainwriting instructions.

3. Hand out paper and pencils to everyone. Form participants into paired groups, with three to five members in each. Have half of the groups follow the brainstorming rules on the instruction sheet to brainstorm different uses for a metal coffee can. Move these groups out of hearing of the other groups before they begin.

4. Give participants in the other half of the groups stacks of index cards and ask them to follow the brainwriting instructions to generate different uses for a metal coffee can.

5. After about ten minutes, ask the participants to add up the number of ideas that have been generated in each group. If there is more than one pair of groups, average the number of ideas for each procedure by adding the number of ideas together and dividing by the number of groups.

6. Announce the results. Brainwriting should have generated approximately four to five times as many ideas as brainstorming if there were four to five people in each group, three times as many ideas if there were three people in a group, and so forth.

Discussion

Discuss with participants why there was a difference in the number of ideas generated. Most people suggest such reasons as apprehension about speaking up, status differences among group members, and interpersonal conflicts. Tell them that, according to research, the major reason for the difference is "production blocking." This simply means that only one idea can be generated at a time during brainstorming; during brainwriting, as many ideas as there are participants can be generated at the same time.

Source
Arthur VanGundy

More Ideas Than You! Brainstorming Instructions

According to Alex Osborn,[1] who created and promoted brainstorming, there are four rules every group should follow:

1. *Criticism of ideas is not allowed.* Separating idea generation from idea evaluation is more likely to lead to a greater number of high-quality solutions.

2. *Freewheeling is encouraged.* Suggest any idea that comes to mind. Most people worry that they have to suggest only logical, practical ideas. On the contrary, some of the best ideas often begin as initially wild and far-out concepts. Even if they cannot be developed into something more workable, their uniqueness often will trigger more unique ideas.

3. *Quantity is wanted.* The more ideas generated, the greater the odds that at least one will be a winner.

4. *Combinations and improvements are sought.* Initial ideas often can be improved by building on them. That is, as group members listen to one another's ideas, they often think of ways to make them more workable or even come up with totally new ideas.

---

[1]Osborn, A. (1993). *Applied imagination* (3rd ed.). New York: Scribners.

More Ideas Than You! Brainwriting Instructions

There are many different brainwriting techniques. The one described below was originally known as "Pin Cards."[2] The steps are:

1. You will be given a stack of index cards.

2. There is to be no talking during this activity.

3. Write one idea on each card and pass it to the person on your right.

4. When you receive a card, read it and do one of three things:

   (1) Use the idea on the card to think of a new idea and write it on a *new* card. Pass *both* cards to the person on your right.

   (2) Modify the idea on the card, write your modification on a *new* card, and pass *both* cards to the person on your right.

   (3) If you cannot think of any new ideas or modifications, simply pass the card to the person on your right.

5. Repeat step 4 until time is called. Try to keep yourself from critically judging any of the ideas.

[2]H. Geschka, G. R. Schaude, & H. Schlicksupp. (1973). Modern techniques for solving problems. *Chemical Engineering,* pp. 91–97.

Promoting and Selling Ideas

Objectives

- To help people learn to promote their ideas
- To help people learn how to write their ideas concisely
- To help people describe the practical applications and advantages of their ideas

Uses

This activity will help participants visualize new ideas and convince others of their value and viability.

Audience

Anyone with ideas he or she wants to have accepted and implemented

Time

Fifteen to thirty minutes

Handouts, Materials, and Equipment

- Paper and pencils for participants
- *Optional:* A word processor

Procedure

1. *Note:* It is assumed that participants have already developed ideas that they would like to implement on the job, but that they do not know how to go about convincing others of their viability.

2. Hand out paper and pencils and instruct the participants to construct scenarios for each idea they would like to see implemented. Tell them that scenarios should be as concise as possible. The more resemblance to a Haiku[3] poem, the better. Their descriptions should be short, in vivid detail, including practical applications of the idea and its advantages. Tell participants that the advantages can, in most cases, be

---

[3]A useful resource is *The Haiku Handbook: How to Write, Share, and Teach Haiku* by William J. Higginson with Penny Carter, published by Kodansha International, 1992.

derived from the criteria that were used to evaluate the idea in the first place. Give them the following example:

Along the busiest highways there are small rooms and small offices where business people can relax and work with computers, make phone calls, send faxes, and access the Internet, just like the rooms provided at airports.

Note that the first part of this scenario describes the idea and that the second part, starting with "where business people . . ." describes the *advantages* of this idea.

3. Have the participants write their scenarios and then form pairs and present them to one another and receive feedback.

4. If there is time, have them practice and receive feedback in more than one pairing.

Discussion

Ask participants to discuss why others seem to resist new ideas. Often, the more revolutionary the idea, the more resistance it will meet because people may have trouble understanding or visualizing it. Help them to see ways that they can use a scenario such as the one they created to kindle the imagination of others, helping them realize the value of the idea and increasing the chances of its being accepted and implemented.*

Source
Robert L. A. Trost

---

*For further reference consult *The Art of the Long View* by Peter Schwartz (President of the Global Business Network). Paperback edition published in 1996 by Doubleday, New York, ISBN 0-385-26732-0.

That's the Worst Idea
I've Ever Heard!

Objectives

- To identify negative responses to new ideas
- To demonstrate how easy it is to think of negative responses
- To compare negative and positive thinking processes

Uses

This activity can be used to illustrate how easy it is to respond negatively to new ideas and how difficult it is to think of positive responses.

Audience

All levels, but especially lower- and mid-level management in small groups

Time

Thirty to forty-five minutes

Handouts, Materials, and Equipment

- Paper and pencils for participants
- A flip chart and markers
- A small calculator

Procedure

1. Divide participants into small groups of four to seven each and give everyone paper and pencils.

2. Instruct each group to brainstorm, without comment, as many general negative responses as possible to new ideas. Suggest that they think of some of the negative comments they have received when they suggested something new to a supervisor or co-worker.

3. Instruct each group to repeat Step 2, but this time to brainstorm positive responses instead.

4. When everyone is finished, have group members count the number of negative and positive responses on their lists. Record the negative and positive numbers from each group and calculate an average response for each type.

Discussion

Most groups find it easier to think of negative responses. Discuss why that may be true. One reason may be that we are more accustomed to receiving negative responses and thus have a larger pool from which to draw. Ask participants whether they have been conditioned to respond to new ideas with an automatic "no," rarely considering a positive side. Discuss why this may be true and have participants share their own experiences.

Variation

Have the groups vote (with applause or a show of hands) for the most creative responses. Award novelty prizes to the winners.

Source
Arthur VanGundy

Think About It

Objectives

- To encourage creative thinking by modeling it
- To motivate participants to increase their creativity

Uses

The activity is helpful to demonstrate how difficult creative thinking can be and to help people examine their curiosity and creativity.

Audience

Team managers and supervisors in groups of three to five

Time

Fifteen minutes

Handouts, Materials, and Equipment

- A flip chart and markers
- Paper and pencils for participants

Procedure

1. Introduce the activity by noting that creativity involves doing things differently, learning from mistakes, and continuing to try.
2. Divide the participants into groups of three to five and ask the groups to consider the following questions, which should be posted on the flip chart:

   What is the oddest thing you have done in the past year that was not done on the job?

   What is the biggest mistake you have made in the past year, and what did you learn from it?

   What new ideas have you tried on the job during the past year, and what were the results?

Discussion

One benefit of this activity is that participants often become more aware that they are not alone in doing odd things, making mistakes, and trying out new ideas. Conduct a large-group discussion of what participants learned about themselves from answering the questions in their small groups, using the following questions as guides:

What have you learned about risk taking and creativity in organizations?

Why are we often reluctant to share the peculiar things we do or our mistakes with others?

What have you learned about yourself from doing this activity?

What reasons do we have for suppressing our creativity on the job?

Source
Rick Kirschner

Tripping

Objectives

- To seek new ideas through imagery
- To practice using imagination
- To become aware of creative ideas in imagery and metaphor

Uses

The activity is helpful to assist in generating new ideas.

Audience

All levels in small or large groups

Time

Thirty to forty-five minutes

Handouts, Materials, and Equipment

- Paper and a pencil for each participant
- A music player
- Music that will become part of the background, such as "The Pines of the Janiculum" in *Pines of Rome* by Respighi (available in the classical music section)[4]

Procedure

1. Instruct the participants to find a comfortable position, one where their bodies will not distract them, such as crossed legs or arms. Have them lie on the floor, if possible.

---

[4]The addition of music is highly effective with this activity, as it helps to block out external distractors, enhances attention and relaxation, and helps stimulate new ideas. The choice of music is *very* important. Participants should not actually listen to the music, but be guided by it.

2. After everyone is settled, dim the lights if possible, and read the following script slowly:

   Close your eyes and begin to focus on your breathing. Just be aware of your breath. Follow the air in . . . and follow it out . . . [wait thirty seconds]. Now count your breaths. . . . Breathing in is 1, . . . breathing out is 2, . . . breathing in is 3, ... Go up to 10 and repeat the process. [Give them enough time to finish the sequence.]

3. Turn on the music and read the following script slowly:

   Now imagine yourself in your favorite place in nature . . . either a place you have been to or would like to go. . . . Take note of the time of year . . . the time of day . . . how the air feels on your skin. . . . Now slowly look around and see what is in your environment . . . plants . . . trees . . . hills . . . rocks . . . clouds . . . sunshine . . . shadows . . . animals . . . the sky. . . .

   You notice a path and begin walking down the path. . . . Now let the music take you. . . . Let the music guide you wherever you would like to go. . . .

4. When the music has ended (after birds and last chord), quickly turn down the sound before it goes into the next piece.

5. Read the following slowly:

   Your journey has ended. . . . Take a moment to remember your experience. . . . Recall what you saw and felt. . . . Now take a deep breath and bring your awareness back to this room. . . . When you are ready, open your eyes and stretch.

6. When everyone is "back," give participants paper and pencils and instruct them to write down their experiences and impressions.

7. Tell them to look for ways how what they experienced relates to their daily lives and to look for solutions to some of their current problems in their experiences.

Discussion

First have participants share their experiences with partners, looking for further insight into ways to solve current problems. Then ask pairs to report their "aha's" and insights to the total group. It is often amazing to participants how many good ideas can come from "getting away from it all" for a few minutes.

Source
Suzanne E. Jonas

Diversity

Divided or Diversified?

Objectives

- To encourage discussion of individual preferences in a nonthreatening situation
- To promote acceptance of differences
- To encourage laughter and playful discussion

Uses

The activity is helpful as a beginning look at diversity in the workplace.

Audience

Any group at any level

Time

Twenty to forty-five minutes

Handouts, Materials, and Equipment

- An assortment of familiar objects, such as balls, Frisbee® rings, whistles, colored paper clips, etc. The objects chosen should have one or more similarities and one or more differences. For instance, the rubber balls should be a variety of colors, sizes, textures, and shapes, such as Koosh® balls, rubber balls, footballs, soccer balls, or tennis balls.

Procedure

1. Divide the items among participants so that each participant has at least five different ones.
2. Instruct the participants to group the articles into two or more categories, according to personal preference.
3. Pair each participant with a partner and have the pairs again devise one system to categorize and group the objects they have.

4. Match two pairs of participants to form a foursome, and have them once again devise one system to categorize their items.

5. If the size of the group permits, match foursomes so that teams of eight devise and categorize the objects using one system.

Discussion

Discuss the challenges faced as the teams grew and changed. Explore with them the reasoning they used to support their various categories. Lead them in discussing sources for the various sorting systems. Then, guide them in discussing how to translate this experience to the workplace as they experience diversity. Ask the following questions:

What can you generalize about diversity in the workplace from this activity?

How do people react when they first must interact with someone new or work with a person who is different from them?

Variation

Mix the team membership each round and then devise a new categorizing system.

Source
Penny Hampton

I Believe

Objectives

- To identify patterns of thinking as part of our diversity
- To compare and contrast ways of thinking and how they influence our interactions with others

Uses

This activity can be used to illustrate how our individual ways of thinking are an important part of our diversity.

Audience

All levels

Time

Twenty to thirty minutes

Handouts, Materials, and Equipment

- 3″ × 5″ index cards for each participant
- Paper and pencils or pens for each participant
- An overhead projector
- Several sheets of blank transparency film for each subgroup
- Transparency markers

Procedure

1. Tell participants that when we hear the word "diversity," we often think of gender or cultural differences. However, diversity also is manifested through our fundamental beliefs. How we were raised as children, what we have been taught, and our own life experiences all contribute to our ways of thinking.

2. Give each participant a 3″ × 5″ card, a sheet of paper, and a pencil or pen. Ask them to write several of their life beliefs on the card. For example:

   - Ninety percent of daily friction is caused by tone of voice.
   - It is not that difficult to be pleasant to others at work.
   - By empowering others, you empower yourself.
   - Do it while you are here; avoid extra trips and save energy.

3. Ask participants to form small groups of two to five members and to share what they have written on their cards with one another. Have them choose one of the sayings that everyone in the group agrees with and one of the sayings that is controversial in the group.

4. Give each group two sheets of transparency film and transparency markers. Ask them to write the statement they all agreed with on one sheet, along with their reasons, and the statement that generated the most controversy on the other, along with their reasons. Tell them to choose a spokesperson to present their findings to the total group.

5. When everyone has finished, have subgroups take turns presenting their sayings to the total group, allowing the group to ask clarifying questions.

Discussion

Lead a discussion of why we sometimes fall into the trap of thinking that others think as we do when, in reality, they have different life experiences and may think in completely different ways. Use the following questions to wrap up the discussion:

How might people's different views influence communication in an organization?

To what extent are the ways we think products of gender? of culture? of upbringing?

How can we use what we have learned to have more effective communication in the future?

Source
Merry C. Buchanan

It's a Man's World After All

Objective

- To recognize how conditioned we are to speaking and thinking in masculine terms

Uses

This activity is intended for use in diversity training or when perceptions of gender differences cause problems in an organization.

Audience

All levels

Time

Thirty to forty-five minutes

Handouts, Materials, and Equipment

- Paper and pens or pencils for each participant
- A flip chart and markers

Procedure

1. Give each participant paper and a pencil or pen. Ask them to brainstorm masculine metaphors used in organizations (e.g., game plan, batting 1000, bench warmer, team player, fumble, pay dirt).

2. Write their examples on the flip chart as they call them out.

3. Ask participants to form small groups of three or four and give each group a "feminine" topic (e.g., shopping, children, clothes, food, home decor, clothing accessories). Ask the groups to generate "feminine" terms that could be used as substitute metaphors within an organization. Groups initially may have trouble coming up with terms for an organization that reflect traditionally "feminine" areas. Help them to start if necessary.

4. When groups are finished, have each group share its metaphors while you write them on the flip chart. Emphasize that organizations are traditionally "masculine." Thus, people do not realize how pervasive masculine language is in the workplace.

Discussion

Ask the group to discuss their reactions to creating and using feminine metaphors, guided by the following questions:

Could feminine metaphors be equally effective?

What problems might people encounter when using feminine metaphors?

How might these problems be overcome?

Source
Merry C. Buchanan

Mandalas

Objectives
- To demonstrate diversity in the workplace
- To teach a method of concentration and focus
- To provide an activity that participants can use again and again

Uses
This activity helps participants to focus during diversity training workshops.

Audience
All levels

Time
Thirty minutes

Handouts, Materials, and Equipment
- A large sheet of paper with a twelve- or fourteen-inch circle drawn in the center for each participant
- Crayons or markers for each participant (crayons are recommended)

Procedure
1. Distribute the paper with the circles and the crayons or markers to participants.
2. Tell participants that they need not be artists to do this activity. Ask them to draw anything they want. Their only restriction is that they must *start in the middle of the circle.*
3. After fifteen or twenty minutes, ask the participants to stop and hold up their papers for everyone else to see.
4. Ask them to discuss the implications of the many types of drawings—the uniqueness of each artist.

Discussion

Share the objectives of the workshop with the participants. Ask for any comments or reactions. Note again how the drawings demonstrate our uniqueness as individuals, even though everyone received the same set of instructions. Point out that it would be a pretty boring world if we all thought and looked alike and that any differences, including cultural and ethnic, can bring a richness to organizations that would not otherwise exist. Elicit from the group the different kinds of contributions that people can make to an organization. Be sure that they appreciate that these very differences enhance an organization's creativity.[1]

Variations

1. Use at the beginning of sessions as a general warm-up activity.

2. Use at any time during a workshop to help participants bring themselves into focus.

Source
Doris J. Shallcross

---

[1]For further information on mandalas, consult the works of Karl Jung or Judith Cornell.

Music Machine

Objectives

- To demonstrate how diverse people with diverse skills and abilities can work harmoniously together
- To illustrate the metaphor of a machine with independent parts all working together to achieve synergy

Uses

When team members fail to take advantage of the diverse resources available in their group, this activity can be useful to remind them of those resources or help with team building. It can also be used to energize a group.

Time

Fifteen minutes

Handouts, Materials, and Equipment

- *Optional:* A recording device to capture the group's results

Procedure

1. Have the participants form a line (it does not have to be a straight line).

2. Ask one of the participants to make a repeating "choo" sound and a continuous up-and-down motion with his or her arms in imitation of a steam locomotive.

3. Instruct a second person to make a different sound and to accompany it with a different movement, but to keep the same rhythm as the first person and to move in unison with him or her, for example, a "whoop" sound accompanied by a hop.

4. Have a third person add a new sound and movement in unison with the second person. Continue this process, with each new person adding on to the previous sound and movement, until everyone is involved at the same time. Remember, the sounds and movements should be continuous and innovative throughout. Each participant's sounds and movements should be inspired by those who have gone before.

Discussion

Guide a discussion with the following questions:

What inspired the various sounds and movements?

What level of harmony and group interaction were you able to achieve?

Would the process be faster and would you attain a higher level of proficiency if you tried the activity again with different sounds and motions? Why or why not?

What would be the results if everyone used the same sound and motion?

What did you accomplish by participating in this activity?

What implications do you see for group diversity?

What would happen if some participants did not do their part or removed themselves from the group? What implications are there for your back-home work team?

Source
Janice Kilgore

Under the Sea

Objectives

- To foster a sense of community within an organization
- To show that although diversity exists in organizations, people's similarities and differences are not always easy to identify or explain

Uses

The activity can be used when there are ethnic- or gender-diversity problems within an organization or for general human-resource training.

Audience

Any, especially groups that are diverse in ethnicity or gender

Time

Twenty to thirty minutes

Handouts, Materials, and Equipment

- A bag of very small sea shells that are similar in appearance. There should be at least one shell per person.
- *Optional:* Unshelled peanuts, corks, chocolates, golf tees, or other small objects similar in appearance instead of shells

Procedure

1. Ask each individual in the group to take one shell from a sack of small sea shells.
2. Instruct participants that they have one minute to study their shells and to become familiar with and find identifying characteristics of their shells.
3. Have participants place their shells in the center of the room (on the floor or on a table).

4. Mix the shells and ask the participants to find their original shells. (*Note:* Usually some confusion takes place; some people locate their shells relatively easily, while others have trouble distinguishing one shell from another. This is part of the process and should be expected.)

5. After participants find their shells, have them return to the large group setting to discuss their experiences.

Discussion

Lead a discussion of the experience, using the following questions:

Was it easy or hard to find your shell? Why?

How are the shells similar? How are they different?

In what ways can shells that appear similar to one another actually differ?

How do people who appear similar actually differ?

What features do shells that appear different from one another have in common?

How are people who appear different actually similar?

How can you use what you have learned in the future?

Source
Merry C. Buchanan

Valuing Diversity[2]

Objectives

- To provide insight into ways to value many types of diversity
- To provide opportunities to explore participants' perceptions concerning different ways of life
- To provide situations that provoke discussion of diversity issues in a group

Audience

Up to twenty-five participants at any level

Time

Sixty minutes

Materials, Handouts, and Equipment

- One copy of the appropriate script for each role player (*Note:* The titles, scripts, genders, locations, and roles may be adapted to meet the needs of any group.[3])

  Just Kidding Around

  Shadow Boxing

  Nonnegotiable

  It's a Long Way to Simi Valley

  Toni and Tom Go Shopping

  Whose Job Is It Anyway?

Procedure

1. Tell the participants that during the activity volunteers will briefly read the roles of individuals in stereotypical situations in order to raise their awareness of certain

---

[2]This activity would not have been possible without the assistance and support of Tom Conlan and Reggie Hobbs of Futuredontics in Santa Monica, California.

[3]The purpose of the scenarios is to raise awareness of the pervasiveness of certain attitudes in our society, even among well-meaning people who are not overtly "prejudiced." It is recommnded that only an experienced facilitator with excellent processing skills use the scenarios as they may seem offensive to some participants.

issues and to discuss them in the group. Explain that, ideally, they will learn ways to handle such situations in real life.

2. Request two to four volunteers to role-play each scenario, depending on the scenario, and on the makeup of the group.

3. Hand out the appropriate role plays and allow people to meet briefly in small groups to read over their scenarios before playing their roles. Say that some situations may seem offensive and/or simplistic, but that it is intentional in order to encourage discussion afterward and not intended to imitate the complexities of "real life."

Discussion for *Just Kidding Around*

Discuss what lessons can be gleaned from this script. Look for the following answers:

People we know and respect can be on welfare.

Economic stereotypes are as damaging as any other.

There may be good reasons why people do not respond as you would expect in a situation.

Expressing oneself before thinking in the workplace (or elsewhere) can create a hostile environment.

Think before you say anything that has the potential to hurt others.

Saying "I was just kidding around" does not excuse offensive remarks.

Discussion for *Shadow Boxing*

Discuss with participants what they would do or say if they overheard the conversation. Possibilities are to speak up immediately, report the incident to a supervisor, or ignore it. Discuss the pros and cons of each possibility. Discuss what they would have done if they were the supervisor and why using any derogatory name can be offensive.

Discussion for *Nonnegotiable*

Discuss the following points:

What would you say if you overheard this conversation?

Why could it be offensive to someone who was not being maligned?

Discussion for *It's a Long Way to Simi Valley*

Discuss the stereotype of geographic prejudice, using the following questions:

What would you say if you overheard this conversation?

What harm can negative impressions about certain neighborhoods have?

Is George as guilty of thinking in stereotypes as Elaine is?

What can be done to overcome these stereotypes?

Discussion for *Toni and Tom Go Shopping*

Discuss the scenario using the following questions:

Do you think this situation is unusual?

Has anyone here ever been followed by a security guard?

How did it make you feel?

What do you think about Toni's comment to the guard?

What would you have done in this situation?

Discussion for *Whose Job Is It Anyway?*

Guide the discussion using the last comment in the script as the point of departure: "What do you think should be done?" Bring out the issue of mandated hiring of minorities.

Variation

Adjust the diversity of the characters and locations in any of the scenarios to align with the background of the group.

Source
Richard G. Wong and Kristin A. Poppenheimer

Valuing Diversity Scenario 1: Just Kidding Around

Characters:

Bob, a white male receptionist for a dental practice

Bill, a white male receptionist for a dental practice

Toni, a black female receptionist for a dental practice

Carla, a white female manager

Bill: (just finishing a call): Hey, this old guy wants his whole mouth restructured on Medicare. Why didn't he take care of it when he was working?

Bob: I'll bet he never had a job.

Bill: Yeah. I'll bet you're right. He didn't sound real bright either!

Bob: I hate the Oprah hour. All of those Medi-Cal queens kill my conversion rate.

Bill: I had a message from one old crone yesterday who was so out of it that she couldn't even leave her phone number. It was so frustrating! These people just don't get it!

Toni: (A black female operator who has been listening to the conversation stands and speaks): I hope it wasn't my grandmother you were talking about. She's retired and has some trouble talking into answering machines with her hearing aid. I told her to call us if she needed a dentist. Her old dentist died and no one took over his practice.

Bill: (flustered): Oh, no. I didn't mean a *regular* person. I was talking about some lazy slob who never had a job. You know, like those welfare people.

Carla: (A manager who has overheard the entire conversation walks over and speaks): When I was young, we were on welfare for awhile. After my father died, my mother needed some help until she could find a job.

Bill: (even more flustered): I'm sorry. I didn't mean to insult anybody. I was just venting.

Bob: I apologize. I didn't mean anything by it. I was just kidding around.

Valuing Diversity Scenario 2: Shadow Boxing

Characters:

Joe, a warehouse employee

Jim, a warehouse employee

Joe: (while shadow boxing with Jim on the work floor): Come on, old man, let's see what you got.

Jim: You're no match for me.

Joe: Come on, let's see what you got.

Jim: That's all right. I don't want to hurt you, son.

Joe: You could never get near me, Fatso.

Jim: Hey, watch your mouth!

Joe: What's your problem?

Valuing Diversity Scenario 3: Nonnegotiable

Characters:
   Two office workers

Two office workers are in the kitchen area during a break.

Worker 1: Are you really thinking about selling your computer?

Worker 2: Yes, I am. It's listed on the bulletin board.

Worker 1: How much are you asking for it again?

Worker 2: Two thousand dollars.

Worker 1: How old is it again?

Worker 2: About a year old.

Worker 1: And you want two thousand dollars for that?

Worker 2: Yeah, I've added a lot of software to the system.

Worker 1: Yeah . . . but two thousand?

Worker 2: That's the price.

Worker 1: How about a thousand?

Worker 2: For all the upgrades, no way.

Worker 1: Fifteen hundred.

Worker 2: For once and for all, no. Stop trying to gyp me down on the price. The computer is selling for two thousand dollars, period.

Worker 1: Hey, I'm offended by that!

Valuing Diversity Scenario 4: It's a Long Way to Simi Valley

Note: It is important to change the locations used in this role play so that they will be relevant to the participants.

Characters:

Elaine, a customer representative

George, a customer representative

Elaine: (speaking to a caller): Yes, that's right. I have a really excellent dentist. (pause) I know that sounds like a rough area down there. I might not want to go down there myself.

George: (thinking out loud) What did she say? I lived near that dental office for eight years. What is she talking about?

Elaine: That's right. I do think this dentist is worth the risk of going down there. Just be careful where you park. Thank you for calling 1-800-555-DENT. (Elaine disconnects)

George: Elaine, why did you say that? Do you know that area? Have you been down there?

Elaine: Well, no, but. . . .

George: Well, I lived there and it's not what you think. It's not Beirut with bombed-out buildings everywhere. There are nice houses, kids, neighbors, dogs, etc. What makes you think it's too dangerous to go there?

Elaine: Well, I heard that there are gangs and stuff and it might be dangerous.

George: Probably no more dangerous than where you live. I wouldn't make assumptions about it and then tell a customer. What has me confused is what picture you must have in your mind of where I live. If the place where I grew up creates such fear in your mind, what do you think of me?

Elaine: I never thought you'd take my remarks so personally. I'm sorry.

Valuing Diversity Scenario 5: Toni and Tom Go Shopping

Characters:

    Toni, a black woman

    Tom, a white man

    Security guard

Toni: (approaching her friend and co-worker): Hey, Tom, it's that time of the year again.

Tom: Gee, are you collecting for the United Way? How much did I pledge?

Toni: No, silly. I'm doing some holiday shopping for my mom, and I wanted to know if you'd like to come along.

Tom: Well, I did plan to buy a nightgown or a dress for my mother. Let's go.

Tom: (surveying the store): Boy, this place is crowded. How am I going to find anything here?

Toni: I'm going to be in kitchen appliances. Women's Fashions is right over there.

Tom: Thanks. (Tom goes in the direction Toni indicated. He passes a security guard who immediately takes notice of him. As Tom walks around each rack, the security guard follows him, very obviously. It takes Tom a moment to notice, but he begins to feel very uncomfortable, so he bends down to tie his shoe. The security guard does the same. Tom loses his balance and tips onto one knee. Toni notices Tom and the guard and walks over to them.)

Toni: I suppose there's a good reason why you're down there. (Gives him a hand to stand up).

Guard: (in an intimidating manner): May I help you, Ma'am?

Toni: No, thanks, just helping my friend here.

Guard: You know this guy!?!

Toni: Yeah. I've worked with him for years.

Tom: (embarrassed, wipes off his pants and says nothing).

Guard: I didn't see you come in together.

Toni: Well, we did. You know, sometimes in other stores, I'm the only person there who looks like me, so they watch me as though I'm going to do something illegal.

Valuing Diversity Scenario 5 (continued)

Guard: (moves away and stops watching them).

Tom: Do you mind if we leave? I really don't want to be in here any more.

Toni: I fully understand.

Tom: Does this sort of thing happen to you often?

Toni: Often enough to be annoying.

Tom: It's awful to be treated this way just because you look different. Now that I've had a brief feeling of what it's like walking in your shoes, I really respect the way you react to things. But I still can't get over this guard. Why did he follow *me*?

Toni: Maybe because you're a guy in the Women's Department. Maybe it's a security guard thing.

Tom: Now if this guy was on the Fashion Police, we'd both be in trouble.

Toni: Whatever do you mean by *we*?

Valuing Diversity Scenario 6: Whose Job Is It Anyway?

Characters:
   Jim and Justin, two white male executives
   Patricia, a white female executive
   Georgette, a black female job candidate

Scenario: Three executives, two male and one female, are interviewing a black female candidate for the second time for an executive's position with their firm.

Jim: We have seen two other candidates a second time. You are the final person we will see before we make a decision.

Justin: Up to this point, each of the candidates has brought excellent credentials and a variety of strengths to the table.

Patricia: We want to thank you for coming in to see us again today. We will make a decision by the end of the week.

Jim: Do you have any questions for us at this time?

Georgette: Yes, I do. Do you mind if I am candid with you?

Jim, Justin, and Patricia: (in unison): Please, go right ahead.

Georgette: What is your commitment to minority hiring?

(Long pause)

Jim: What do you mean?

Georgette: Well, while I was touring your company, I noticed that there are very few minorities or women.

Justin: Well, we are very committed to minority hiring.

Patricia: I agree, and the fact that you've made it through two interviews and are one of three applicants in the running for this current position bears this out.

Georgette: Yes, but does your company actively recruit minorities?

Justin: Recruit?

Valuing Diversity Scenario 6 (continued)

Georgette: Yes, place ads in minority publications, send representatives to job fairs—that sort of thing.

Jim: No, up to this point we have not felt it necessary to do that. We will definitely keep that in mind for future reference.

Georgette: Thank you all for the opportunity to interview with you (leaves).

Jim: Can you believe the nerve? Whose idea was it to bring her back for a second interview anyway?

Justin: That's not important. What's important is that she's a troublemaker. Imagine what she would have done at an executive board meeting.

Jim: If she feels that strongly about diversity, why doesn't she start her own company?

Patricia: I think you two missed the point completely (long pause).

Justin: Well then, why don't you enlighten us?

Patricia: The point is that we could do more. We could send our representatives to minority-oriented job fairs. We could advertise in minority publications and tell our recruitment agency that we are committed to a diverse workforce. (Turning to the audience) What do you think?

Energizers

Box of Life

Objectives

- To encourage new thinking
- To increase awareness of one's norms and values
- To evaluate and implement training results

Uses

This activity is useful on the last day of a training session.

Audience

Any number at any level

Time

Five to ten minutes

Handouts, Materials, and Equipment

- Several sheets of paper and a pencil for each participant
- Any small container such as a box or hat

Procedure

1. Hand out paper and pencils to all participants. Note that we all sometimes use inspiring mottoes or clichés to help lift our spirits during difficult times.

2. Instruct each person to write an inspiring motto or cliché on a piece of paper. Tell them to try to relate the motto to the theme of the training session. Give them some examples:

   For a seminar on time management or team building, you might write: "Don't put off until tomorrow what you can do for your team today" or, for a motivational seminar, you might write: "It's not the size of the dog in the fight, but also the size of the fight in the dog."

3. After everyone has finished writing a motto or cliché, show the box or hat and ask the group to suggest names for it, such as "Fund for the Members of the Board of Directors."

4. Pass the box around the room and ask each person to put his or her motto into it.

5. After the box has been returned to you, promise the group that in a few weeks' time you will send them all of the mottoes, assembled in some way. Say that this way everyone will remember the training session for a longer period of time. (*Note:* This could be as simple as typing the mottoes on several sheets of paper and stapling them together or as elaborate as creating a small scrapbook for each participant.)

Discussion

After everyone has deposited a motto in the box, read the contributions aloud and ask the group members to discuss what they mean. Tell them that the person who wrote the motto should allow others to try to figure it out before jumping in with the answer. You can also wait until the end of the training session to discuss the mottoes. (*Note:* Be sure you follow through on your promise to collate the mottoes and send them to everyone.)

Variation

Divide the participants into small groups. Give each of these groups a number of mottoes, and let them discuss them. Then, have each group select the most original one and give an award for it.

Source
Arie Maat

Go Team! RAH!

Objectives

- To build team spirit in a work group
- To celebrate work-team successes
- To stimulate and energize work teams to discuss training issues

Uses

This activity helps to energize a group in the early stages of team building or to celebrate the end of a successful team-building session.

Audience

Lower and middle management or frontline employees

Time

Thirty to sixty minutes

Handouts, Materials, and Equipment

- Poster board and markers for each group
- Pompoms, megaphones, noise makers, team shirts, team jerseys, etc., for each group

Procedure

1. Have participants form small groups and tell them they are the new spirit leaders for their work teams (like school cheering squads).

2. Have each team make up words and gestures for a team chant or cheer, and choose colors, a mascot, a logo, and a name. Tell them that their choices should reflect the team's relationship to the job. Give them poster board and markers to post their logo and name.

3. Give groups about fifteen minutes to come up with cheers, etc., and then have each team perform for the rest of the group.

Discussion

After the demonstrations, lead the group in debriefing what they saw and how each group demonstrated current team issues, creativity, pride, energy, or any topic of interest. Discuss how they can keep their level of energy back on the job.

Variations

1. Offer incentives for the top three cheering demonstrations.
2. Offer prizes for various categories, such as creativity, team spirit, etc., so that each team is a winner in some category.

Source
Penny Hampton

Hands-On Networking

Objectives

- To help participants meet one another
- To add energy to a workshop

Uses

The activity is especially useful after lunch, after a break, or near the end of a day to perk up a group.

Audience

Any, the larger the group the better

Time

Five to ten minutes

Handouts, Materials, and Equipment

- A watch with a second hand

Procedure

1. Welcome the participants. Mention that networking is one of the major benefits of a workshop, conference, or convention.

2. Ask everyone to stand up, empty their hands of any objects, and push their chairs under the tables or back against the wall to free up some space.

3. Give participants any number of seconds to shake hands with everyone else in the group. (*Note:* In general, the larger the group, the more time you should allow. However, there should be time pressure and participants must feel as if there is not enough time.)

4. Say "Go!" and let everyone know how much time is left once or twice during the activity. (*Note:* To paraphrase Parkinson's Law, "No matter how much time people have, they will use it.")

5. Call time and ask participants to return to their seats.

Discussion

Use the following questions to discuss what happened during the activity:

What observations can you make about others in the group? Did other people seem organized, energetic, systematic, chaotic? Were they having fun?

Did anyone try to organize the group? If so, how well did it work and how did you feel about that?

Did you learn anything that will carry over to the remainder of the program?

Variation

For a little added excitement, participants can be told to shake hands with two other people simultaneously whenever possible.

Source
Robert Alan Black

Hugs and Kisses

Objectives

- To energize a group involved in a lengthy training session
- To lighten the mood of an intense training session
- To set a tone at the beginning of a training session

Uses

When group energy is lagging after lunch or late in the day, this intervention can perk everyone up.

Audience

Any number at any level

Time

Five to ten minutes, depending on group size and room configuration

Handouts, Materials, and Equipment

- Several bags of Hershey's® Hugs and Kisses chocolates
- Several baskets

Procedure

1. Explain to the group that you want to ensure that the group is feeling supported and nurtured.
2. Say that when times are rough in a group, hugs and kisses can help. Imply that there will be physical contact, but do not overdo it so that anyone is offended or put off.
3. When people are at the peak of anticipation, produce one or more baskets filled with candy.
4. Pass the baskets around and let the joy of chocolate permeate the atmosphere.

Discussion

Lead a discussion of changes in the group as the result of something as simple as chocolate candy. Ask:

What effect did giving out candy have on the climate of the group?

How might this affect the training to follow?

Source
Penny Hampton

Meet and Greet

Objectives

- To provide a positive team-building environment for a large group
- To help create a relaxed atmosphere
- To provide a fun and enjoyable experience

Uses

This activity is helpful for energizing a group or as a warm-up activity.

Time

Fifteen minutes

Audience

Groups of more than twelve participants at any level of education and experience

Handouts, Materials, and Equipment

- A recording of high energy Latin music. (*Note:* Select music with long cuts to provide continuity without long breaks between songs.)
- An amplification device to permeate the room with the sound of heavy bass
- A room with plenty of unobstructed space

Procedure

1. Have participants form two lines in diagonally opposite corners of the room. One of the lines should have one more person than the other. Put people who will be likely to set the tone of fun at the beginning of each line and encourage them privately to dance to the center of the room when they begin. Tell them to think of an atmosphere similar to a limbo line or conga line with laughter, shouts of joy, clapping, and revelry. Ask them to encourage the rest of the group to join in the fun.

2. Start the music and ask the first participant from each line to move to the center of the room, shake hands, and then go to an unoccupied corner to form new lines. Encourage dancing and lively behavior.

3. Continue the process until only one participant has not gone to the center, greeted someone from the other group, and then rejoined his or her own group in a new corner.

4. Have that person move to the front of the line for his or her group, and repeat the process so that everyone greets a different person this time. Then ask participants to be seated for discussion.

Discussion

Discuss with participants how this activity made them feel and whether they are more or less ready to start learning than they were previously. (*Note:* It is helpful to schedule a short activity that requires remaining in small groups to help maintain the energy level.)

Variations

1. For very large groups, form four lines, one in each corner of the room. Have four participants meet simultaneously for a group hug or greeting.

2. Change the mood by selecting other types of music with high-energy beats, such as jazz, rhythm and blues, etc. Schedule different activities afterward, depending on the music; for example, soulful music for a thought-provoking activity or to set the mood for the day's activities, classical for inspirational problem solving, Big Band music for activities associated with the immediate past, folk or square dance music for harkening back to simpler times, and high-energy modern music with overtones of futuristic sounds to plan for the next century.

Source
Janice Kilgore

What's My Line?

Objectives

- To help energize participants during a lull in training
- To allow participants to learn little-known facts about their teammates or co-workers
- To see how observant participants are about one another

Uses

This activity can be used throughout the course of a training program as a small break or diversion. It is designed to be broken into small segments, used at various times until the activity is completed. It is ideal for training sessions for new teams.

Audience

Appropriate for any training group, at any level of the organization, whether participants think they know one another well or have just met for the first time

Time

Three to five minutes for each segment; number of segments depends on the size of the group

Handouts, Materials, and Equipment

- One 3" × 5" index card per participant
- A pencil for each participant

Procedure

1. Give one 3" × 5" index card and a pencil to each participant. Tell the participants to write something about themselves that they feel no one else in the group knows: a hobby, interest, event, or accomplishment, but not a personal secret or something they would not want others to find out.
2. When everyone has written on his or her card, collect all the cards.

3. At various points in the training, take a break from the course content, pull out three or four of the cards, and read them aloud to the class one at a time. Ask if anyone can guess whose card it is. After several guesses, ask the writer to reveal himself or herself and go into more detail about what is written on the card. After three or four cards, return to the course content. Repeat at various intervals throughout the training until all cards have been read.

Discussion

Include a wrap-up discussion of this method of getting to know one another at the end of the session. Ask if participants feel ready to resume training.

Variation

Make the activity into a competition by awarding points to those who guess correctly. Obviously, this is only fair if people really do not know one another.

Source
Richard Whelan and Robert Merritt

Evaluation

Benchmarking Team Feelings

Objectives

- To quantify participants' feelings about their team and/or their work
- To facilitate discussion and recognize improvement over time

Uses

This activity is good for evaluating team climate or for use in a team-building session.

Audience

Intact work teams only

Time Required

Twenty to thirty minutes, depending on the size of the team and the length of the discussion

Handouts, Materials, and Equipment

- Enough large, colorful self-adhesive dots (about one-inch in diameter) in two different colors for each participant to have one dot of each color
- A pen for each participant
- A flip chart and markers
- Pushpins or masking tape
- Two copies of a *Benchmarking Team Feelings Chart* drawn on a flip chart with the vertical axis labeled: "How I Feel About My Work" and the horizontal axis labeled: "How I Feel About the Team" (a sample is shown on page 142).

Procedure

At the beginning of the session:

1. Welcome the participants after they are seated and review the objectives of the workshop or meeting. Briefly describe the goals of the activity to the group and what they will be asked to do.

2. Review principles or guidelines they wish to have for their time together and post them on the flip chart. (*Note:* Be sure they list "respect others" as one of the items.)

3. Give everyone one adhesive dot (all of the same color) and ask them to put their names or initials on it.

4. Now ask the participants to rate their feelings about the team and their feelings about their work. Tell them to write this down somewhere so that they will not be tempted to ignore their actual feelings later.

5. Have the participants plot their feelings on the chart by placing their dots at the intersection of the two lines that best represent how they feel. Remind them to be honest, as that will benefit the team the most.

6. After all participants have placed their dots on the chart, ask each participant to describe why he or she placed the dot in that position. Other members of the group may ask clarifying questions, but they may not judge or criticize. Remind everyone that the intent is to listen to one another's feelings and understand why they feel the way they do. Agreement or consensus is *not* the goal.

7. This chart serves as a benchmark for the group prior to the session. Post it on a wall.

At the end of the session:

1. Repeat Steps 2 through 6 using a different color dot.

2. Look for trends (ideally, improvements) in the way the participants feel about the team and their work. This chart shows the impact of the session and generally helps people feel good about the results. Post it beside the other chart.

Discussion

Be certain that each participant has an opportunity to express his or her feelings openly and that all participants follow the meeting principles and respect other people.

Discuss the charts, focusing first on the pre-session chart. Use the following questions to draw out their responses:

What did you observe when the team first put up the dots?

Were you surprised by the placement of any particular team member's dot? Why?

Was it difficult to put your dot in the place you felt it belonged? Why?

Did you feel particularly close to any other team member? Was that a surprise to you?

Next, focus on the second chart, asking the following questions:

What changes do you see in the second chart?

How do those changes make you feel?

Are there any surprises on the chart? What are they and why were you surprised?

How did it feel to put your dot on the chart the second time?

Do you feel closer to any team member(s) now than you did when we started?

What can you do to continue to improve the team back on the job?

Variations

1. The same chart can be used for multiple sessions with the same group. Use different dot colors and create a key to track both the participants' and the group's progress over time.

2. Team members can be given a third dot of a different color and asked to plot where they would ideally like to be. Discuss ways to close any gaps that exist.

Source
Mary K. Wallgren

Benchmarking Team Feelings Chart

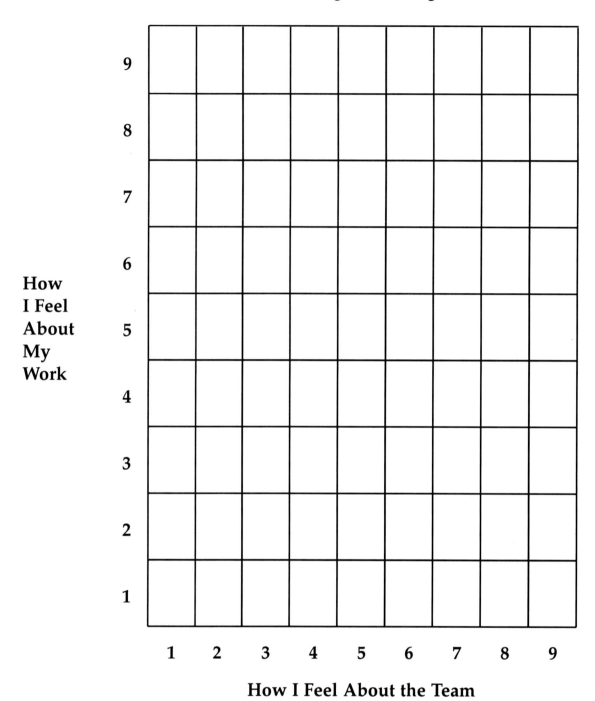

How
I Feel
About
My
Work

How I Feel About the Team

Phrase Phases

Objectives
- To promote more creative evaluation of training sessions
- To allow participants to express their creativity

Uses
The activity is useful during or after a training session, as a supplemental evaluation, for clarifying expectations, or during team building.

Audience
Any level in groups of three to five

Time
Twenty to thirty minutes

Handouts, Materials, and Equipment
- Paper and pens or pencils for each participant
- One *Phrase Phases Listing* for each participant
- A flip chart and markers for each group

Procedure
1. Break participants into groups of three to five members each, give each group a flip chart and markers, and distribute paper and pencils and one copy of the *Phrase Phases Listing* to each participant.
2. Ask everyone to scan the list of phrases. Have one member from each group select one phrase to use as a stimulus to evaluate the training session. For instance, the phrase "the sound of a fire popping" might suggest: "There were a lot of ideas 'popping' out during the session."
3. Have groups choose scribes to record each evaluation on the flip chart.

4. Have the other group members repeat the process, selecting a phrase, thinking of an evaluation comment, and writing it on the flip chart until everyone has contributed. If time is available, go through the process again to generate even more comments.

5. Tell the groups to review all their comments, write a summary statement, and share with the other groups.

Discussion

After each group has shared its summary statement, use the following questions to discuss the evaluation experience:

Were the evaluation comments more creative than those created using more traditional methods such as written forms?

Did the comments differ more within groups or between groups?

In what other situations might this evaluation method work? Where would it not work as well?

Did some groups tend to have different areas of focus? If so, why was that?

Variation

Use all the comments to develop a written evaluation questionnaire. Have the participants rate their agreement with each question using a five-point Likert scale, where 1 is "strongly disagree" and 5 is "strongly agree."

Source
Arthur VanGundy

Phrase Phases Listing[1]

1. The sound of a fire popping
2. Wide-mouthed toasters
3. Kleenex™ unfolding one at a time
4. Pop-up books
5. Knee socks
6. A January night that engraves itself on the mind
7. The last crumpled leaf on an oak tree
8. Sorting clean laundry
9. A soft pillow
10. Lumberjacks
11. Country auctions
12. Walking sticks
13. The yellowing pages of old books
14. Fishing
15. Rain hitting a tin roof
16. Clouds quickly moving by
17. Kittens
18. International relations
19. Marketing a new medicine
20. Secret doors
21. Lovers whispering
22. New-fallen snow
23. Smelling an ocean breeze
24. A grandfather clock ticking
25. Football and basketball
26. Receiving forgiveness
27. Polishing shoes
28. Pulling teeth
29. Arguing with a friend
30. A smokey production line

[1]Source: Barbara Annkipfer. (1990). *14,000 things to be happy about*. New York: Workman Publishing.

Pieces of the Puzzle

Objectives

- To disseminate information submitted by team members
- To create a nonthreatening way to share feedback about critical issues
- To illustrate metaphorically the importance of input from all team members

Uses

This activity is best for providing feedback from surveys and other team evaluation tools or for a subtle approach to team building.

Audience

All levels in groups of ten to twenty

Time

Ten to twenty minutes

Handouts, Materials, and Equipment

- One blank puzzle kit for each category you have chosen
- A flip chart and markers for each group
- Results from evaluation sheets filled out in advance by participants, or any training terms or other pertinent words and phrases you wish to use

Procedure

1. *Prior to the training session:* Determine the general evaluation categories you wish to use. These may be from questions on evaluation forms filled out earlier by participants or topic headings in the training workbook, or whatever you wish. Categorize the words and/or phrases and write them on separate puzzle pieces, one category per puzzle, e.g., leadership, teamwork, or decision making.

2. *At the end of the training session:* Have participants form small groups and give each group one puzzle. Explain that each puzzle, when assembled, contains all the information specific to the training topic. (For instance, a puzzle on leadership might include pieces with such words as: influence, persuasion, task, power.)

3. Have each team assemble its puzzle, and then ask someone from each group to list on a flip chart the words or phrases that were on the pieces.

4. Ask the groups to use the words or phrases they have listed to discuss whether the training session met all the needs put forth on the evaluation forms or whether they learned all of the terms under each topic in the workbook, or whatever the purpose of the activity: discussion, explanation of terms, or so forth.

Discussion

Use the following questions to segue into the next training topic or activity:

Did putting together the puzzles help energize the evaluation process?

What effect does sharing the results have on the overall evaluation process?

How can the groups make a smooth transition from this activity to another training topic?

Variations

1. Time the groups as they assemble puzzles and offer incentives to the quickest teams.

2. Mix the puzzle pieces among groups to enhance teamwork analysis.

3. Have individuals in groups write major concepts learned on the puzzle pieces. Then complete Steps 3 and 4 of the Procedure above.

Source
Penny Hampton

Showing What We Have Learned[2]

Objectives

- To review key points from the workshop content
- To determine what needs to be reinforced
- To explore additional learnings that were not planned

Uses

Use this activity at the end of a training seminar to review material, energize groups, discover missing or additional learnings, and to reinforce the importance of content on-the-job. The primary goal of this activity is to challenge the participants while providing them an opportunity to review what they have learned and compare their learnings with those of the other participants.

Audience

All levels

Time

Thirty to forty-five minutes

Handouts, Materials, and Equipment

- Crayons or markers for each participant
- Large poster board or newsprint paper for each small group

Procedure

1. Tell participants that studies show that the majority of people take in most information through their eyes, yet most people rarely use drawing, sketching, or diagramming to express their ideas and understanding. Most people could be called visually illiterate. Say that this activity will provide an opportunity to enrich their learnings through visual memories.

---

[2]A suggestion to trainers using this activity is to photograph some samples of complex billboards or collect visuals from newspapers or magazines to show participants. Also, take photos of the billboards from the session, after obtaining permission from the participants, to use later with other groups.

2. Divide participants into small groups of three or four people and assign them the task of designing and creating a billboard that captures ten to twelve key points from the program through the use of both words and drawings.

3. Tell them that all members of each group must be involved in both the design and the creative production of the billboards. Stress that aesthetics are not a major factor nor is artistic skill. Tell participants that they can use symbols, geometric shapes, stick figures, or arrows. Answer any questions and hand out newsprint paper and crayons or markers to each group.

4. Explain that you also expect each member of the group to take part when they present their billboards to other groups when they are finished.

Discussion

As groups present their billboards, have other participants comment on anything that has been left out or added. Be certain that everything from the workshop has been covered well.

Variation

Assign the groups to create a television commercial or a newspaper or magazine advertisement.

Source
Robert Alan Black

Stand by Me

Objectives

- To experience the evaluation process
- To energize participants to engage in the evaluation process at the end of a training event

Uses

The activity can be used for any type of evaluation, such as evaluating training sessions, ideas, or group decisions.

Audience

Any level in groups of four to fifteen

Time

Ten to fifteen minutes

Handouts, Materials, and Equipment

- Five sheets of flip-chart paper
- Red, blue, black markers
- Masking tape
- Paper and a pencil for each participant

Procedure

1. *Prior to the workshop or meeting:* Tape five sheets of flip-chart paper side by side along a wall, leaving about three feet between sheets. Use a *blue* marker to write a large number "1" on the sheet of paper to the far left, a *red* marker to write a large number "5" on the sheet of paper to the far right, and a *black* marker to write "2," "3," and "4" in order on the remaining sheets.

2. Hand out paper and pencils and have participants form small groups or work together to create a list of evaluation questions for the workshop or training session. (*Note:* Questions must be phrased so as to be answered on a five-point Likert scale.)

3. When each group has a list of nine or ten good questions, have them stop working, give their lists to you, and stand up. Tell participants that the blue number "1" on the first sheet represents a "cold" or negative response, the red number "5" represents a "hot" or positive response, and the numbers between are lukewarm, depending on how close they are to the blue or red numbers.

4. Read the evaluation questions from each group. Instruct participants to stand in front of the number that best represents their responses for each question as you read it. For instance, if the question is: "To what extent did the seminar meet your expectations?" participants who believed that it completely met their expectations would stand by or near the number "5." Those who felt it did not meet their expectations at all would stand by or near the number "1," and those who felt less strongly would stand next to one of the remaining numbers.

5. Read the questions and record the number of participants standing by each number for each question, multiply that number by the numeral on the paper, and add up the totals. For example, if three people are standing in front of "1," two in front of "2," and two in front of "4," the total score would be 15 [(3 × 1) + (2 × 2) + (2 × 4) = 3 + 4 + 8 = 15].

6. Repeat the process until all of the questions have been asked and evaluated and add up the total evaluation scores.

Discussion

Discuss the experience, using the following questions:

How did this experience compare with using more traditional evaluation forms?

Were you ever tempted to stand where the largest number of people was standing? What did you do?

Do you think that this approach is as objective as more traditional anonymous evaluation methods?

In what ways could this approach be used to improve group evaluations?

Variations

1. Use an existing evaluation, rather than create new questions.

2. Have participants individually complete an evaluation questionnaire and score it prior to the session and see whether the results are the same. If not, discuss what happened and why.

3. Repeat some of the questions at random intervals to see whether people "vote" the same way. Discuss the differences.

Source
Arthur VanGundy

Getting to Know You

Cartoon Time

Objectives

- To help participants start to get to know one another
- To make introductions more fun

Uses

Use this activity as an icebreaker or for climate setting when participants do not know one another.

Audience

Teams, small- to medium-sized groups

Time

Five to ten minutes

Handouts, Materials, and Equipment

- One or two cartoons from a newspaper per participant
- Masking tape

Procedure

1. Prior to the meeting, place the cartoons on a table or attach them to a wall where everyone can see them easily.
2. At the beginning of the meeting, give everyone time to look for a cartoon that fits him or her well. Have participants select one cartoon each and integrate it somehow as they introduce themselves to the rest of the group.

Discussion

Wrap up the introductions by asking what aspects of participants' personalities were revealed that would not usually come out from a simple introduction. Discuss how the activity felt to participants and whether they found it more helpful to learn about others in this way and why.

Variations

1. Distribute the cartoons randomly and have people think of something to say about themselves that fits the cartoons they receive.

2. Each participant can introduce the person on his or her right using either his or her own cartoon or the other person's cartoon.

Source
Roger J. Syverson

Comic Relief

Objectives

- To allow participants to get to know one another
- To help create an open and informal atmosphere
- To increase group cohesion for a training session

Uses

This activity is appropriate for any training session in which participants do not know one another.

Audience

All levels, but especially useful for groups of twenty or more

Time

Ten to fifteen minutes

Handouts, Materials, and Equipment

- One cartoon panel from a comic strip per person

Procedure

1. *Prior to the session:* Cut several cartoon strips into individual panels. Choose strips with two, three, or four panels to ensure that the total number of panels matches the number of participants in the group.
2. At the beginning of the session, give each participant one cartoon panel.
3. Instruct the participants to move around the room to find people with panels from the same comic until they have created a whole cartoon strip and to remain in groups.
4. When all participants have formed small groups based on their completed cartoon strips, have one person from each small group read the group's cartoon for the large group.

Discussion

Lead a discussion of the experience as a getting-acquainted activity, using the following questions:

Did you find variations that seemed to be the next segment of your cartoon strip? How did you work with others to determine what was the correct panel?

How many new people did you meet while circulating? Was it less stressful to meet new people when you had a purpose?

Source
Melinda M. Morris

Let's Connect!

Objectives

- To show well-acquainted participants the surprise and delight possible from making new connections
- To provide an enrichment experience at the beginning of a two- to three-day work session

Uses

The activity is useful for setting the stage for making connections and generating new ideas.

Audience

All levels in groups of twenty or fewer

Time

Twenty to thirty minutes

Handouts, Materials, and Equipment

Personal items from each participant

Procedure

1. Ask participants to take out all pictures from their wallets, purses, or briefcases. Remind them that this may include their driver's license or pictures of someone else.

2. Instruct the participants to find partners and to talk to one another about their pictures, explaining who is in the pictures, how long they have owned them, what significance they have to them, and where and when they were taken.

3. Tell them to reassemble in the large group and have each participant present his or her partner to the group by using the partner's pictures. Ask them to highlight new things they have discovered about one another and what the two of them have in common. Allow about one minute per person.

4. After everyone has finished, discuss with the group whether there were any surprising new connections made with teammates, despite the fact that they thought they knew one another well.

Discussion

Share the concept of "surprising new connections" as the foundation for generating ideas. Explain that unique ideas are often developed when one "connects to" or "borrows from" a seemingly unrelated topic. Draw out examples from the group of people doing this naturally every day by unconsciously allowing their minds to wander; for example, thinking of an idea in the shower. Help participants see ways that they can harness their creative energy consciously through making new connections when they are back on the job.

Source
Leslie Berger

Let's Get to Know One Another

Objectives

- To help participants to get to know one another
- To create a nonthreatening environment in which everyone can participate

Uses

This activity is designed for use with new small groups of four to five participants each.

Audience

Any number of participants who do not know one another well

Time

Ten to fifteen minutes

Handouts, Materials, and Equipment

- A copy of the *Let's Get to Know One Another Handout* for each participant
- An overhead transparency of the *Let's Get to Know One Another Handout*
- An overhead projector
- Pens or pencils for each participant

Procedure

1. Welcome the participants and note that people learn most effectively in a supportive and familiar environment.
2. Introduce the activity as a way for people to get to know one another better.
3. Distribute a copy of the *Let's Get to Know One Another Handout* and a pen or pencil to each participant.
4. Tell the participants that they have ten minutes to mill around the room, asking others all of the questions on the handout and filling in people's names and answers. Ask them to interview as many people as possible and to ask each person at least two different questions. Tell them *not* to volunteer information, but to wait

to be asked. (*Note:* Ideally, every person would speak to every other person in the room and have answers to all questions.)

5. At the end of ten minutes, display the overhead of the questions and go around the room and have people tell the group any new information they have learned about fellow participants. Post answers on the transparency sheet.

Discussion

Ask participants whether the type of information they have collected will make it easier for them to work together as a team. Lead a discussion of ways they can use what they have learned about one another during the program.

Variation

The facilitator can develop his or her own list of questions, either directly relevant to the workshop topic or some combination of related and unrelated information.

Source
Robert Alan Black

Let's Get to Know One Another Handout

Instructions: Take a few minutes to get to know the other people in the room. Using the following list of questions, mill around the room and ask each person in the group at least *two* different questions during the next ten minutes. Fill in the person's name and answer after each question.

Questions:

1. Tell me something no one else in this group knows about you.

2. What is something that annoys or frustrates you about today so far?

3. What was one of life's most embarrassing moments for you?

4. Name one thing that you value and appreciate.

5. How would you like your great-grandchildren to describe you?

6. Name one thing you are especially proud of about your organization.

7. Name one thing you really enjoy doing in your job.

8. If money were no object, what would you do?

9. What quality do you respect most in others?

10. If you ran for office, what office would you choose?

Light, Medium, or Heavy

Objective

- To encourage participants to make self-disclosure statements

Uses

This activity is useful to loosen up a group and helps them to become better acquainted.

Audience

Participants in a group meeting

Time

Fifteen to twenty minutes

Handouts, Materials, and Equipment

- A set of stimulus cards prepared for each group prior to the meeting according to the instructions in the *Light, Medium, or Heavy Trainer's Notes*
- 3" × 5" cards and markers for making stimulus cards
- Tables for each small group to play the game

Procedure

1. Have participants form small groups of three to five members. Hand out a set of stimulus cards to each group. Instruct participants to shuffle the cards and place them face down in the middle of the table.

2. Read the following rules for the activity to the participants:

The first player picks up the top card and reads the word written on it out loud. He or she then makes a revealing personal statement related to the word. This statement should not take more than one minute. For example, if the word is "lemonade," the person might say: "When I was about nine years old, my mother was always asking me to take lemonade to my grandfather so he wouldn't have to get up himself. I used to spit in the glass before pouring the lemonade because I resented having to wait on my grand-

father. When he died recently, he left me quite a bit of money. I feel very guilty about what I did back then."

After each statement, the other members of the group are to hold up one, two, or three fingers to indicate how personally revealing the statement was. A light or flippant statement is worth one point. An emotional, embarrassing statement is worth three points. Statements in the middle are worth two points. Different people may assign different numbers of points to the disclosure.

The person who made the statement then counts the total number of fingers that are raised and writes his or her score on a scorecard. For example, if four other players agree that a statement is worth three points, the person would receive twelve points.

If you do not want to talk about a particular stimulus word, you may pass and receive no points for the round. The next participant may then use that card or pick a new card. Keep track of your own scores and go around until I tell you to stop.

3. Depending on the time available, have participants continue for three to five rounds or until all the cards have been used a certain number of times. Be certain that each participant has an equal number of turns. Call time and ask for high and low scores in each group, showing the most and least revealing information.

Discussion

Discuss participants' reactions to this activity. In particular, ask the high- and low-scoring people why they were more and less comfortable about sharing personal information with the others. Also, discuss whether the activity helped them learn more about one another and how this information could be helpful in dealing with one another in the future.

Source
Sivasailam "Thiagi" Thiagarajan and Raja Thiagarajan

Light, Medium, or Heavy Trainer's Notes

Instructions: Make a deck of cards by writing words or phrases either related or unrelated to some problem facing the group on 3″ × 5″ cards. Create identical packets of about twenty cards for each subgroup.

Some sample stimulus words and phrases for a team-building workshop are: lemonade, role, ground rules, goal, waste of time, computers, budget, beeper, midnight, window, money, short people, yellow, wishful thinking, fishing expedition, sharp focus, resolution, sunshine, discipline, and leadership. Note that some words are related to the topic and some are irrelevant; some are bland and some are potentially embarrassing.

Picture That

Objectives

- To help participants learn more about one another
- To creative a climate conducive to creative thinking

Uses

The activity works well as a small-group icebreaker or for getting acquainted.

Audience

Any level

Time

Ten to fifteen minutes

Handouts, Materials, and Equipment

- One copy of the *Picture That Sheet* for each subgroup
- A flip chart and markers

Procedure

1. Divide participants into small groups of four to six members each and give each subgroup a copy of the *Picture That Sheet*.

2. Tell them that each group member is to review all of the pictures and select the one that best describes him or her.

3. When everyone has chosen a picture, tell participants to take turns describing themselves to other group members *without revealing which picture they have chosen,* but using imagery from the picture. Tell them to be as specific as possible; for example, a person who selected the picture of the bridge might describe himself or herself as "someone who can bridge the gap that exists between marketing and R&D."

4. Request that other group members listen to the descriptions carefully and then try to guess which picture best represents that participant. Continue until everyone has had a turn.

Discussion

Ask all participants to discuss their reactions to the activity, especially what strengths were identified that might help improve group or organizational functioning. Ask them what descriptions were predictable and if there were any surprises. Write on the flip chart what they will do differently back on the job now that they know more about one another's strengths.

Variations

1. Cut up the sheet of pictures and give pictures to group members at random. They then must use whatever picture they received to describe themselves.

2. Have group members select two pictures each and use them both for the self-descriptions.

Source
Arthur VanGundy

Picture That Sheet

Puzzling

Objectives

- To begin interacting as a group
- To learn one another's names and a few interesting facts

Uses

This activity can be used as an icebreaker or for getting acquainted in a small group.

Audience

Lower- to mid-level employees, especially newly-formed groups

Time

Ten to fifteen minutes

Handouts, Materials, and Equipment

- One puzzle template or a small, blank jigsaw puzzle for each group

Procedure

1. *Prior to the workshop:* Photocopy one puzzle template for each group onto card stock, if possible. Cut each puzzle into pieces indicated by the lines and keep puzzles in separate containers of some type.
2. Form participants into small groups and distribute the pieces for one puzzle to each group. Tell group members to divide the pieces equally among themselves, with each group member receiving at least two pieces.
3. Next, tell group members to write their first names on one puzzle piece and a fact about themselves, such as profession, hobby, where born, marital status, number of children, or whatever, on the other piece.
4. Now have group members assemble their puzzles, reading the information as they place the pieces together.

Discussion

Ask all participants to discuss their reactions to the activity, using the following questions for guidance:

What leadership patterns emerged in your group?

Did you learn new information about one another?

How can what you learned be applied during this workshop? On the job?

Variations

1. If the group members already know one another, ask them to write facts about themselves that others might not know.

2. Distribute puzzle pieces randomly to members of the large group and have them form small groups. Each group then completes what it can of the puzzle using the information it has and must interact with other groups to trade for missing pieces.

Source
Arthur VanGundy

Who Are These People?

Objectives

- To help participants begin to get to know one another
- To begin to create an environment in which everyone will participant freely without feeling threatened

Uses

This activity is designed for getting acquainted with other participants.

Audience

Any

Time

Ten to fifteen minutes

Handouts, Materials, and Equipment

- One copy of the *Who Are These People? Questionnaire* for each participant
- An overhead transparency of the *Who Are These People? Questionnaire*
- An overhead projector and transparency markers
- Pencils for participants

Procedure

1. Introduce this activity as a way for the participants to begin to get to know one another. Explain that people tend to learn most effectively in a supportive and familiar environment.

2. Give each participant a copy of the questionnaire and tell the group that they will have ten minutes to find out the answers.

3. Give a reminder when there are two minutes left, and again when one minute is left. Allow another minute if needed, and then call time.

4. Ask them to give you answers to the questionnaire while you write them on the overhead transparency for everyone to see.

Discussion

Ask the participants whether having this information or information like this would make it easier for them to work together as a team during the workshop. Discuss why this is true for the particular workshop purpose.

Variation

Customize a list of questions or information relevant to the training topic or 50 percent content related and 50 percent general interest.

Source
Robert Alan Black

Who Are These People? Questionnaire

Instructions: To become better acquainted with other members of the group, move around the room and find people who match the following descriptions. Write their names after each description.

Try to interview as many people as possible in the time allowed, rather than using just one person who fits many criteria. Find people who:

1. Played varsity sports in school

2. Has/Had an unusual pet

3. Loves classical music

4. Has lived in a foreign country

5. Has/Had an unusual collection

6. Speaks a foreign language

7. Plays a musical instrument

8. Is a mystery story fan

9. Is a M*A*S*H fan

10. Scuba dives or snorkels

Goal Setting

Goal Pictures

Objectives

- To help clarify individual goals
- To demonstrate how goals can be improved using creative thinking

Uses

The activity can be used for any general training, especially involving goal setting, or for training in creative thinking.

Audience

All levels

Time

Twenty to thirty minutes

Handouts, Materials, and Equipment

- One color picture of any scene unrelated to the training topic for each participant
- One flip chart (or whiteboard) and markers
- Several sheets of paper and a pencil for each participant

Procedure

1. Describe the objectives of the activity and give each participant several sheets of paper and a pencil.

2. Instruct each participant to write down three individual work-related goals (e.g., "to achieve higher performance ratings" or "to improve communication with subordinates"). Give them time to do this.

3. Distribute one picture to each participant. (*Note:* The pictures may be cut from magazines or come from any source, so long as they are unrelated to participant goals.)

4. Ask the participants to write detailed descriptions of everything they see in their pictures. Model this activity for the group using the flip chart or whiteboard. For

instance, if a picture shows the sun setting over some hills with birds circling around, you might list the following:

Birds are flying in the sky.

The birds are flying in formation.

There are clouds that appear to be drifting.

The sun is glowing red and reflected onto the clouds.

The sun is setting over some hills in the distance.

Nearby trees have lost many of their leaves.

5. Give them time to write their descriptions. Then tell them to use what they have written as a stimulus to generate ways to improve or otherwise modify each of the goals they wrote previously. Model this using the following goal: "To improve communication with subordinates." For instance:

Go on trips with subordinates (birds are flying in the sky).

Have subordinates participate in outdoor team-building activities (birds are flying in formation).

Have subordinates take Effective Listening workshop (clouds appear to be drifting).

During conversations with employees, summarize their feelings and content of the discussion to show understanding (reflected in the clouds).

6. Have the participants use this process to generate at least two ideas to improve each of their goals, taking other pictures if needed.

7. Encourage individuals to share some of their goals with the large group.

Discussion

Some people seem to have particular trouble diverting their focus from a specific topic. Discuss the effectiveness of this technique for generating more creativity, using the following questions:

Was it difficult to use unrelated stimulus pictures to generate ideas? Why or why not?

What new insights did you gain about your goals?

Based on this activity, have you found ways to modify your original goals? Which ones?

What new goals did your pictures suggest?

Source
Arthur VanGundy

New Hires

Objectives

- To demonstrate the value of goal setting prior to making decisions
- To emphasize the importance of setting goals

Uses

The activity is useful to teach goal-setting skills for organizational or team purposes or for setting personal goals.

Audience

Any participant at any level

Time

Thirty minutes

Handouts, Materials, and Equipment

- Paper and pens or pencils for each participant
- A flip chart and markers

Procedure

1. Give each person paper and a pen or pencil and then read the following to the group:

   In order to make effective decisions, groups must first analyze problems and then set goals. It is important to avoid personal prejudice or political motivations when setting goals.

2. Divide the participants into small groups of three to five members. Tell each group to imagine the following scenario:

   You are on the search committee choosing a new employee for your department. As a group, determine the top five criteria by which you will screen applicants. Your group must reach a consensus on the five most important qualifications for the new employee.

3. After about fifteen minutes, when all groups have finished, have each group share its five criteria and post them on the flip chart.

Discussion

Use the following questions to guide a discussion of the activity:

In what ways would a search for a new employee be simplified by establishing goals beforehand?

How could decision making become bogged down if no goals were set?

What are some other situations in your work or personal life when you could accomplish more by setting goals ahead of time?

Does goal setting help to clarify a task? If so, how?

Source
Merry C. Buchanan

Personal Mission Statement

Objectives

- To identify professional goals and objectives
- To help participants see how their professional goals are similar to or different from their organization's goals
- To develop specific objectives to accomplish participants' professional missions

Uses

The activity is designed for use for general training or new-employee training.

Time

Forty-five to sixty minutes

Handouts, Materials, and Equipment

- One *Personal Mission Statement Worksheet* and a pencil for each participant
- A flip chart and markers

Procedure

1. Give one copy of the *Personal Mission Statement Worksheet* and a pencil to each participant.
2. Briefly discuss with the group ways in which *organizational* mission statements help clarify values and set specific goals to achieve organizational objectives. Explain that a *personal* mission statement should reflect both one's role in the organization and one's goals in one's current position.
3. Have the participants complete the first question on the worksheet. When they are finished, discuss as a group who the organization's stakeholders are and who is directly affected by their success or failure and why. List the stakeholders on the flip chart.
4. Have the participants complete the second question on the worksheet. When they have finished, list and discuss the personal and professional values they hold in common.

5. Based on the lists of values and stakeholders, instruct each participant to use the worksheet to create a personal mission statement for his or her own job. Encourage participants to be concise and to list specific objectives they feel will help them be successful.

6. When everyone has finished, ask group members to read their personal mission statements aloud to the group.

Discussion

Use the following questions to help summarize the activity, raise any related issues, and discuss organizational goal setting at the individual, group, and organizational levels.

What is the purpose of a mission statement?

Does your organization have a mission statement? If so, what does it say?

Who holds a stake in your professional and organizational success? In what way?

What are some common values in your organization that affect the way you conduct business?

How can you use a personal mission statement? How can you use it to focus on what is really important in your daily activities?

Did you have objectives that you must meet? How will you seek to meet them?

Which objectives are the most important for you to succeed in your personal mission?

How can your personal mission contribute to the organization's success?

Source
Melinda M. Morris

Personal Mission Statement Worksheet

1. Who holds a stake in your professional and organizational success? In what way?

2. What common values do you share with other organizational members?
   Personal Values:

   Professional Values:

3. Create a personal mission statement that reflects your role in this organization. Be sure to think about who has a stake in your success and the values that might be affected by your mission. Set specific objectives for yourself, but be concise. An effective mission statement is one that can be remembered easily.

S.M.A.R.T. Basketball

Objectives
- To evaluate and choose group goals
- To motivate participants to consider group goals in a more structured way

Uses
This activity can be used for general training sessions, team building, or any group evaluation task.

Audience
All levels, in groups of four to seven

Time
Twenty to thirty minutes

Handouts, Materials, and Equipment
- Six small office wastebaskets or cardboard boxes
- Five Nerf® balls for each participant or sheets of colored paper wadded into balls
- One copy of the *S.M.A.R.T. Goal Setting Handout* for each participant
- A flip chart and markers
- Masking tape

Procedure
1. *Prior to the meeting:* Write the words "Specific," "Measurable," "Achievable," "Relevant," and "Timely" in large block letters on separate sheets of paper. Make the first letter in each word about twice the size of the other letters, in red or a color different from the rest of the letters. Tape the sheets to five wastebaskets, one sheet per wastebasket.
2. Place the wastebaskets in a row in front of the group so that the letters read S.M.A.R.T. Explain that this activity is designed to help the group evaluate and choose goals.

3. Have the group brainstorm a list of at least ten team goals or other goals relevant to their group or organization (or use an existing list) and write them on the flip chart.

4. Help them to discuss the goals for clarification and to make any needed changes. Be sure that everyone has basically the same definition of each goal.

5. Distribute five Nerf® balls (or colored paper balls) and one copy of the *S.M.A.R.T. Goal Setting Handout* to each participant.

6. Have the participants read the "S.M.A.R.T." criteria and answer any questions they may have about their intended meaning. Point out that the first letter of each word on the wastebaskets represents those five criteria, S.M.A.R.T.

7. Read the first goal that is listed on the flip chart. Tell participants to evaluate it by simultaneously tossing balls into the wastebaskets representing the criteria it meets. For instance, if a participant believes a goal is "specific," "achievable," and "timely," he or she would toss three balls, one into each respective wastebasket.

8. After the goal has been "evaluated," count the number of balls in each basket and record the total on the flip chart.

9. Repeat Steps 7 and 8 for the remaining goals. Declare the best goals to be those with the highest total points.

Discussion

Discuss this technique for setting goals and evaluating them, as well as the rating for the goals by using the following questions:

How well did this activity work for evaluating your goals?

Did you notice a tendency to toss balls into baskets already containing balls? Why did that happen?

Did you take this form of evaluation as seriously as more traditional approaches? Why or why not?

In what ways could this approach improve group evaluations?

Did everyone understand the criteria? If not, what could have been done to increase your understanding?

Variation

Continue the evaluation process by examining the criteria receiving the least number of "votes" for each goal. Try to determine why the criteria cannot be met and use this information to brainstorm how to achieve them, assuming that the group believes that the goal is achievable.

Source
Arthur VanGundy

S.M.A.R.T. Goal Setting Handout

Instructions: Use the following list of criteria to evaluate each of the group's goals. Consider whether each goal is:

Specific

Does it specify exactly what is desired? Is it clear?

Measurable

Can it be measured objectively? Will success be obvious?

Achievable

Is it realistic to expect your group to achieve this goal?

Relevant

Does the goal pertain to the team (or organizational) mission and values?

Timely

Is this goal appropriate at this particular time?

Icebreakers

Boxes of Your Life

Objectives

- To focus the participants on the content of the workshop
- To challenge their concepts of "being in boxes"
- To help participants explore the positives and negatives of their boxes

Uses

Use this activity to focus, introduce, reintroduce, or reinforce content of the workshop.

Audience

All levels

Time

Thirty to forty-five minutes

Handouts, Materials, and Equipment

- Masking tape for making eighteen-inch square outlines on the floor (one for each participant)
- *Optional:* Larger square pieces of colored paper, if masking tape cannot be used
- A flip chart and markers

Procedure

1. *Before the participants arrive:* Outline one eighteen-inch box on the floor for each person, using masking tape.
2. When everyone has been seated, talk briefly about the topic of creativity and how we experience blocks to our creativity in the workplace.
3. Ask the participants to find a box to stand in for awhile and to think of "boxes" they may be in on the job or in the workplace. Give them three or four minutes to think about it.

4. Ask people to pair up with someone near them (without leaving their boxes) and share their thoughts about ways that each of them lives in a box at work. Partners can clarify, but not make comments at this time. Give the pairs eight or ten minutes to share.

5. Now ask them to take turns suggesting how their partners can step out of their boxes. Again, allow eight or ten minutes.

6. When everyone has made suggestions, ask for some volunteers to share their ideas and post them on the flip chart.

7. Now have participants physically remove and destroy the boxes they have been standing in and return to their seats.

Discussion

Have the participants discuss their reactions to and learnings from the activity. Lead a brief overview of the key points they have learned, discussing how overcoming boxes in our jobs or our workplaces can be truly beneficial for our creativity.

Source
Robert Alan Black

Corporate Jester

Objectives

- To stress the importance of challenging assumptions
- To help foster a fun and humorous environment
- To poke fun at ourselves and our organizations, as court jesters did

Uses

Use the activity as an enjoyable warm up for creativity and to help break down some hierarchical barriers within an organization if multiple levels are represented in the group.

Audience

Any size intact work group or management group, in subgroups of four to seven people

Time

Twenty to twenty-five minutes

Handouts, Materials, and Equipment

- Pens or pencils and paper for each participant
- A flip chart and markers for each subgroup

Procedure

1. Break participants into small groups of between four and seven people and have each group pick a scribe to record ideas on a flip chart.

2. Hand out paper and pencils or pens and tell each participant to list some corporate success factors or best practices or policies from his or her organization, such as "pay for performance" or "just-in-time shipping."

3. When they have finished, tell them to discuss as a group what they have written and then record the best two or three ideas on their flip charts, leaving room under each statement.

4. When the groups are finished, tell them to *reverse* their statements, for example "pay for non-performance" or "non-pay for performance," and to create as many supporting arguments for one of the reversed policies as they can. Give them some examples, such as "Our people will be less stressed"; "Recruiting will be easier"; "Managers will make more money and do less work the higher they go"; "We'll have to spend less time with performance reviews"; etc. Have them write the statements on their flip charts.

5. After ten or fifteen minutes, have the groups report their results, showing what they have written on the flip charts to the large group and explaining their reasoning.

Discussion

Use the following questions to debrief the activity:

What were some of the purposes of the original court jester?

What value is there to questioning some of our closely-held corporate beliefs?

What salient points were made about your organization or work group? What action will you take when you return to the job?

What other questions did this activity spark for you?

Source
Dave Gunby

Handshaking

Objectives

- To warm up the participants and start their creative juices flowing
- To demonstrate that there is much creative energy in the group
- To energize the group

Uses

Use this activity to warm up a group in a nonthreatening way with no materials in a short time.

Audience

At least ten participants at any level

Time

Fifteen to thirty minutes

Handouts, Materials, and Equipment

None

Procedure

1. Ask the participants to stand up and form circles of ten or more people each. If there are fewer than twenty-five people, have them form only one circle.
2. Talk briefly about nonverbal communication and body language and that messages can be just as clear as through words.
3. Tell the participants that they are to develop a creative, unique handshake without using any verbal communication whatsoever.
4. Choose a starting place in the circle and tell that person to create a unique handshake with the person on his or her left and have that person pass the handshake on to the person on his or her left until the handshake has gone around the circle. Each person may contribute ideas in turn, so the handshake will evolve as it goes around the group.

5. As the group handshake is being passed around, verbally encourage and praise the group. Challenge them to be as creative as they can and not to limit themselves to using their hands only.

Discussion

When the group has finished, have the first person identify the differences between the handshake as it began and the handshake at the end. Comment on the creativity that exists in the group and lead a discussion of the results, using the following questions:

How did it feel to do this activity nonverbally?

Did you enjoy learning and creating a handshake? If so, why? If not, why not?

What did you learn from taking part in this activity?

What did it demonstrate about the creative talents of the participants in this group?

What analogies can be drawn to the workplace?

How could the activity be used back on the job to enhance creativity?

Source
Robert Alan Black

KNOWU Cards

Objective

- To help participants meet, mix, and mingle with others and get to "know u"

Uses

The activity is helpful for large groups who are meeting for the first time or for diverse groups, such as members of a work team and their guests at a social event.

Audience

Groups of thirty or more, or vary the activity for smaller groups

Time

Thirty to sixty minutes

Handouts, Materials, and Equipment

- At least three different KNOWU cards, ten copies of each card for thirty participants
- Pens or pencils for each participant
- *Optional:* Small gifts for winners

Procedure

1. *Prior to the session:* Copy equal numbers of at least three of the KNOWU cards onto colored card stock. For thirty participants, ten copies each of three cards are required.

2. Give one card and a pencil or pen to each participant.

3. Explain that they are to find people who have had the experiences listed on their cards, ask the people to sign the appropriate squares, and continue until their cards are completed. Explain that each person can only sign a particular card once. Therefore, when they finish, each of them will have twenty-five different signatures or initials on his or her card.

4. Ask them to stand up and circulate among the other participants now to complete their cards.

Discussion

Discuss how the activity felt and whether people learned anything new about one another that they can apply in the future.

Variations

1. Set a time limit, for example, twenty minutes, and award prizes to the first few people who turn in their cards. If there is a tie, determine the winner from the bonus question at the bottom of each card. Be sure to tell people whom to give the cards to when they are finished and to number cards in order of receipt.

2. Enough prizes can be available for everyone, with people picking from the prize selection in the order in which cards are turned in.

3. If time is short, rather than fill the entire card with names or initials, each person can complete one row horizontally, vertically, or diagonally.

Source
Mary K. Wallgren

KNOWU Card 1

Instructions: Have as many squares signed or initialed as possible. Each person may only sign your card one time!

Like to Rollerblade	Read science fiction novels	Ride the bus to work	Baked cookies within the month	Have taken a snow vacation
Kept this year's New Year's resolution	Work on most holidays	Am the youngest child in family	Use the Internet	Write letters to friends at least four times a year
Drink more than two cups of coffee a day	Planted a garden this year	Watch fireworks on the 4th of July	Married more than ten years	Plan to leave town for Christmas holidays
Have been to the Grand Canyon	Speak a foreign language	Play a musical instrument	Like to hike in the woods	Have a flag flying outdoors at home
Attended private school	Do volunteer work	Am a soccer parent	Watched a parade in person this year	Have a pet cat

BONUS: List the seven dwarfs.

KNOWU Card 2

Instructions: Have as many squares signed or initialed as possible. Each person may only sign your card one time!

Like Chinese food	Read romance novels	Have a collection of more than fifty "things" (e.g., spoons)	Have three or more rose bushes	Have taken a second honeymoon
Have been to a major league baseball game this year	Have a pet dog	Was in a school play	Subscribe to the *Wall Street Journal*	Play in a sports league
Like to play cards	Plant a garden	Have been camping within the year	Married less than one year	Have grown children who do not live at home
Have been to Las Vegas	Am a vegetarian	Write poetry	Grew up in this town	Love to do crossword puzzles
Worked at McDonald's	Have lived outside the U.S.	Am the oldest child in family	Jog ten miles per week	Live in an apartment

BONUS: Sing (or say) the first verse to *The Star-Spangled Banner.*

KNOWU Card 3

Instructions: Have as many squares signed or initialed as possible. Each person may only sign your card one time!

Have flown a plane	Read the paper every day	Own a condominium	Have twin boys	Have vacationed outside the U.S.
Have performed in front of a group	Am a gourmet cook	Attended a military school	Have made homemade candy	Like to ride a mountain bike
Like the opera	Have more than ten house plants	Like to bowl	Have four or more children	Have never ridden on a train
Have been to Mount Rushmore	Like to sing	Am a chocoholic	Have written a book or would like to	Have been to a professional football game
Swim at least once a week	Have taken a vacation by the beach	Vote in every election	Fixed turkey for Thanksgiving dinner	Have a pet other than a cat or dog

BONUS: List the last ten presidents.

KNOWU for the Holidays 1

Instructions: Have as many squares signed or initialed as possible. Each person may only sign your card one time!

Use real pine boughs to decorate	Leave tree up full twelve days after Christmas	Have hung Christmas stockings	Usually attend Midnight Mass	Have a Christmas necktie
Will have goose for Christmas dinner	Have seen a Santa	Received a Christmas gift in the mail	Bake fruit cake	Have mistletoe hanging
Received at least fifteen holiday cards already	Have a child in a holiday program at school or church	Have finished holiday gift shopping	Will celebrate Hanukkah	Like egg nog
Own a Christmas sweatshirt	Will have ten or more people for holiday dinner	Have children who still believe in Santa Claus	Have an artificial tree	Will fly during the holidays
Have read *A Christmas Carol*	Serve wassail for holidays	Bought yourself a special gift for the holiday	Have your kids' pictures taken with Santa	Watched a Christmas special on TV this year

BONUS: List Santa's eight reindeer.

KNOWU for the Holidays 2

Instructions: Have as many squares signed or initialed as possible. Each person may only sign your card one time!

Cut down a real tree	Attended *Nutcracker* ballet	Have New Year's plans	Baked Christmas cookies	Stay home for the holidays
Kept this year's New Year's resolution	Have to work over the holidays	Have an Advent wreath	Celebrate Hanukkah	Write a form letter for holidays
Do not send Christmas cards	Put tree up after Thanksgiving	Put up luminaries	Hung lights on a tree outside	Plan to leave town for the holidays
Attended school Christmas program	Make Tom and Jerry's	Include a photo with your Christmas card	Dress up as Santa	Open gifts on Christmas Eve
Know three wise men	Set up a manger	Made a Christmas wreath	Go shopping the day after Christmas	Have a wreath on your front door

BONUS: List the gifts from "The Twelve Days of Christmas."

KNOWU for the Holidays 3

Instructions: Have as many squares signed or initialed as possible. Each person may only sign your card one time!

Put money in a Salvation Army kettle	Will give your boss a Christmas gift	Use a Christmas savings account	Made a holiday gift	Plan to have holiday party or open house
Watch the *Grinch* on TV each year	Made a wreath with fresh greens	Decorate outside with lights	Like Christmas music	Send holiday cards overseas
Make New Year's resolutions	Uses the phrase "Bah Humbug"	Have gone caroling	Eat fruit cake	Wrote a holiday form letter
Decorate your office at work	Drink Tom and Jerry's	Tour the neighborhood looking at holiday lights	Wait until Christmas morning to open gifts	Peek at Christmas gifts
Use an Advent calendar	Do charity work over the holidays	Have more than one Christmas tree	Celebrate Kwanzaa	Know what *Tannenbaum* means

BONUS: Sing the first verse and chorus to *Jingle Bells*.

Implementation

Five Double You's

Objectives

- To structure the implementation process
- To ensure successful implementation

Uses

Use the activity for implementing ideas from training, strategic planning, or training in creative problem-solving skills.

Audience

Any intact work teams of four to seven people responsible for implementing ideas

Time

Twenty to thirty minutes

Handouts, Materials, and Equipment

- Flip charts and markers for each group

Procedure

1. Have participants form into their work teams, four to seven members each. Ask each group to think of an idea to implement. (*Note:* This can be an actual project of an intact group or any idea familiar to all group members, such as implementing a "Casual Friday" social hour or implementing a new product or marketing strategy.)

2. Give each group a flip chart and markers. Ask participants to appoint scribes in each group to write each of the following questions at the top of a separate sheet of flip chart paper:

   What are we going to implement? Why?

   Who is going to implement it? Why?

   Where are we going to implement it? Why?

   When are we going to implement it? Why?

3. Instruct each group to discuss and answer the "What?" question (the definition and description of what is desired) and write their answers below the question. Have them respond to the "Why?" question at the bottom of the page, that is, "Why do we need to implement this particular idea?"

4. Move around the room to check that each group has the idea and have the groups do the same thing for the "Who?" "Where?" and "When?" questions, filling in the answers to "Why?" at the bottom of each sheet.

5. Ask the groups to review all of their responses to the questions and modify any answers as needed. Tell them to pay particular attention to obstacles that might be encountered and how to overcome them.

6. Next, have each group use what they have written to design an implementation action plan. Each plan should detail the steps needed for implementation ("What?"), the people involved ("Who?"), where implementation will occur ("Where?"), and the time and duration of each activity ("When?").

Discussion

Each group should report on its plan to the other groups, who can help them look for anything that has been left out. Lead a wrap-up discussion with the following questions:

How did responding to the "Double You" questions affect the implementation plan you designed? (*Note:* Look for the answer that the process was more thorough and efficient.)

Were there activities you might have forgotten if you had not used this approach?

Which question was most useful? Why?

Would the value of the questions vary from situation to situation? What are some examples?

What, if anything, would you do to improve this process?

When will you use it again?

Source
Arthur VanGundy

Mental Rehearsal

Objectives

- To formulate action plans
- To practice implementing new ideas and techniques
- To become aware of any areas needing adjustment or improvement

Uses

The activity is intended to assist in helping a group to implement new ideas or techniques.

Audience

All levels, individual to large group

Time

Fifteen minutes

Handouts, Materials, and Equipment

- A music player
- Some music to block out external distractions and help participants focus[1]
- Paper and pencils for participants
- A flip chart and markers

Procedure

1. Give everyone a piece of paper and a pencil. Have participants relax in their chairs. Dim the lights, if possible, and turn on the music.

---

[1]Music is highly effective with this activity, but the choice of music is very important. Participants should not actually listen to the music, and therefore, it must not be recognizable or distracting. Possible choices are: slow, New Age pieces such as "Comfort Zone" or "Spectrum Suite" by Steven Halpern or "Music for Relaxation" by Jim Oliver. The best choice is "Cloudscapes," available from Music & Medicine, 5A Meadow Oak Lane, South Deerfield, MA 01373.

2. When everyone is settled, read the following slowly:

Close your eyes and focus on your breathing. Be aware only of your breathing. Follow the air in . . . and follow it out . . . [wait thirty seconds]. Now count your breaths: breathing in is 1 . . ., breathing out is 2 . . ., breathing in is 3 . . ., breathing out is 4. Count your breaths to breathing out at 10. . . . Now start over and repeat the sequence. [Wait an appropriate time.]

Now imagine yourself back at work. You are feeling energized, confident, and eager to implement the new ideas you have learned. See yourself carrying out these new plans. Imagine every detail. . . . How will you start? . . . Whom will you talk with? . . . How will you interact with and educate others? . . .

See yourself accomplishing the task confidently and successfully. . . . See others responding positively to your plan and actions. . . . Feel the excitement of success and completion. . . . If there are any problems, see yourself handling them with ease and confidence. . . .

Now move ahead one month. . . . You are at work . . . your new plan is in place and running smoothly and effectively. . . . Do you see any areas for adjustment or improvement? . . . If so, make a mental note now. . . . Allow yourself to enjoy your success. . . .

Now let the images fade. . . . Bring all of your experiences back to the present. . . . Take a slow deep breath. . . . Slowly open your eyes. . . . Write down anything that you want to remember about your experience.

Discussion

Have the group share their experiences in pairs. Expand to small groups if appropriate, and then have the large group help you list on the flip chart ways they can be successful in implementing new ideas in the workplace.

Source
Suzanne E. Jonas

Sandwich to Go

Objectives

- To create awareness about the complexity of implementation
- To demonstrate the need to consider contingency plans during implementation

Uses

Use this activity at lunch time during project management or brainstorming training when teaching people how to implement their ideas.

Audience

Any number at any level

Time

Thirty to forty minutes

Handouts, Materials, and Equipment

- A flip chart and markers, whiteboard and markers, or overhead projector with blank transparencies
- Paper and pencils for each participant
- Enough food for each participant to make a sandwich (e.g., sliced bread; deli meats such as ham, chicken, pastrami; lettuce; tomato slices; onion slices; pickle slices; mayonnaise; ketchup; mustard)
- Knives, forks, plates, and napkins

Procedure

1. At the lunch break, lay out the food and utensils for participants. Then read the following to the group:

   Implementation is an often overlooked problem-solving or training activity. Although we may develop good solutions to problems, they will be of little value if not implemented correctly. The same holds true for learnings from training sessions. It is not enough to attend the sessions; learnings also must be applied in the work setting.

2. Instruct the participants to line up at the buffet table and make a sandwich using the food available.

3. After everyone has made a sandwich and is seated, give them permission to eat while they work.

4. Tell the participants to pretend that they have a new friend from Mars who has never heard of a sandwich.

5. Ask them to write down every activity involved in making the sandwich so that their sandwich-clueless friends could produce the same result. To do this, they must be very specific and list every activity involved. Give as an example that they may not write something like "Put a piece of meat on a slice of bread," but must describe how to pick up the piece of bread and where to place it, the particular type of meat to use, how to arrange it on the bread, and so on.

6. When everyone has finished, ask at least two volunteers to read their descriptions aloud and record them for all to see.

7. If time is available, have people work in pairs to evaluate one another's instructions.

Discussion

Say that most people underestimate the complexity of implementation tasks and that we take many steps and activities for granted. We also tend to underestimate how much time is required. Discuss the concept of being specific and detailed enough for someone else's benefit. Ask the following questions to start the discussion:

What were the major differences between the two descriptions recorded? Was one more specific than the other? Did they provide sufficient detail?

What did you learn by doing this activity?

What was most surprising about it?

What specifically had you taken for granted when writing your instructions?

Variations

1. Have the participants draw a flow chart showing the sequence of each activity, plus contingency decision points (e.g., is the meat correctly centered on the bread? If yes, go on to the next step; if no, then align the edges of the meat with the edges of the bread and center it).

2. Descriptions can be written first and given to partners to make the sandwiches exactly as described before eating them.

Source
Arthur VanGundy

Taking Ownership of New Ideas

Objectives

- To identify steps of the innovation process
- To help group members feel comfortable with new ideas

Uses

Use during any training session in which new ideas, procedures, or technologies will be presented or an organization is in the process of implementing new ideas, procedures, or technologies.

Audience

All levels

Time

Forty-five to sixty minutes

Handouts, Materials, and Equipment

- One copy for each participant of the *Taking Ownership of New Ideas Worksheet*
- Pencils for participants
- A flip chart or large whiteboard and markers

Procedure

1. Give each participant a copy of the *Taking Ownership of New Ideas Worksheet* and a pencil.

2. Briefly discuss that new ideas come from an attempt to solve existing needs or problems. Have participants fill out the first three questions on their worksheets, describing the new idea, the problem it seeks to address, and ways it can help organizational effectiveness.

3. When they are finished, list their answers on the flip chart and clarify them. Then ask them to list ways that the change will effect them personally. After they have done this, make a list on the flip chart of the ways their jobs will be affected and discuss them briefly.

4. Now say that although sometimes we feel uncertain or threatened by new ideas, there are ways to "take ownership" of them and make them work.

5. Tell participants to fill out the "Taking Ownership" section of the worksheet (questions 4, 5, and 6). When everyone has finished, list some of the benefits they have seen on the flip chart. Brainstorm other benefits to all of them from embracing the new idea or procedure.

Discussion

Lead a discussion of the experience using the following questions as guides:

How does it make you feel when new ideas are proposed? Why?

What questions do you still have about the new system?

How can this idea be tailored to suit your specific needs?

Does seeing the benefits instead of the problems of a new process or idea help you to get used to it more easily?

What ways can you think of to make the new idea or process part of your normal routine back on the job?

Source
Melinda M. Morris

Taking Ownership of New Ideas Worksheet

Instructions: This worksheet is designed to help you think about the benefits of a new idea, process, or technology for your job. It is important to understand the need for the new idea, the benefits it provides, and ways to "take ownership" of a new system to make it work for you.

Name: _____

1. Briefly describe the proposed new idea, process, or technology.

2. What need does the new idea seek to fill, or what problem does it seek to correct?

3. How would this idea help organizational effectiveness?

Taking Ownership of the Idea

4. Based on your own and the group's ideas of how this might be a useful idea, how can you take "ownership" of the idea and make it work for you?

5. Which parts of your job will be made easier or more efficient if you implement this idea?

6. What questions or concerns do you have that must be addressed before you implement this idea?

Interviewing

Baptism by Fire

Objectives

- To ward off the negative effects of group interviews
- To empower participants during interviews
- To demonstrate the potential positive aspects of interpersonal interaction

Uses

This activity helps to practice the skills needed when an individual is being interviewed by a group.

Time

Thirty minutes

Audience

Any size group at any level

Handouts, Materials, and Equipment

- Paper and a pencil for each participant
- A flip chart and markers
- One copy of the *Baptism by Fire Interviewing Suggestions* for each participant

Procedure

1. Tell participants that being interviewed by a group can be one of the most grueling experiences in their professional lives. Say that the questions that people in the group ask often have little thought given to them and achieve minimal results, so the opportunity is perfect for them to prepare beforehand to achieve a good impression. Explain that this activity is designed to prepare them for such an experience.

2. On the flip chart, draw a picture of a box with three trap doors. Tell them that when they are in a tough situation, such as a group interview, to think of the magic box with three methods of escape.

3. Ask them to think of three ways that a magician might escape from a box without anyone being aware of the escape. Ask for their ideas, but steer them toward the answers that they could use coverings or obstructions or diversions to keep the audience from noticing an escape. Tell them that they will need to be adept at verbally escaping from questions that are off-topic or may present them in a negative light.

4. Hand out paper and pencils and ask them to determine how they want to "appear" after such a verbal escape. Tell them to think creatively and to be unconventional, writing their ideas down on paper. Ask them to share their thoughts with the rest of the group.

5. Now ask everyone to think of ways to escape the audience's questions by covering, obstructing, or diverting their attention. Ask them to write down three questions and the answers they could use that would serve the purpose during a group interview. Write the following question on the flip chart as an example of a diversion: "Let me answer that question with this question: Is it better to do well on a task and have everyone know, or is it better to do poorly and only a few people know?"

6. Have them brainstorm benefits to the company from hiring them. Write their answers on the flip chart. Help them think of things to say that bring the audience back to these benefits when any of the following questions are asked:

How do you view yourself in this company?

How might you achieve success in this company?

What lasting effects might there be from hiring you?

What role do you see yourself assuming here?

7. Help the group come up with other potential questions and devise some answers that cover, obstruct, or divert the questioners' attention back to the benefits of hiring them. Practice for long enough that everyone feels comfortable with the technique.

8. Hand out the *Baptism by Fire Interviewing Suggestions* and discuss them with everyone. Remind them to use a mental picture of the magic box to remind them of some techniques to use to stay in control of the interview the next time they are being interviewed by a group.

Discussion

Wrap up with a discussion of how conducting oneself during a group interview is much like a magic trick. Check what the group has learned from this activity and what they would do differently when going to another group interview. Discuss the specific approach to take, using the following questions:

How should you act in relation to the group?

In what ways can you determine what a group might be feeling about you?

Should you act as if you are already hired or in a deferential manner?

Should you act with great self-confidence or take the posture that you are feeling your way through the experience?

What methods can you use to create a bond with each member of the group? Are there certain words to avoid or include?

Source
Janice Kilgore

Baptism by Fire Interviewing Suggestions

- Acknowledge each person's presence as he or she enters the room.
- Take turns giving full eye contact to each member of the group.
- Do not move your eyes or body too swiftly, to avoid giving the impression of being deceptive or dishonest.
- Never allow your eyes to be downcast.
- Avoid negative situations from your past by preparing a brief statement that diverts their attention from the past and helps them look forward to the future.
- Do not try to play mind games with members of the group or appear to be a smart aleck, but be knowledgeable about their company and the specific position you are applying for.
- State positive aspects of the company and position and show how you can bring a new approach to the position that can be beneficial to all involved.
- Be flexible and open to situations and insert humor through tasteful interjections, avoiding jokes.
- If possible, shake hands with all members as you leave.
- Gather your belongings and leave with a confident posture.

Empowered to Know

Objectives

- To provide a basic outline for drawing out responses from job candidates
- To help people explore their experiences that are relevant to future jobs
- To help both parties to an interview "own" the process

Uses

This activity can be used to train people how to be interviewed or to help interviewers hone their skills.

Audience

Any size group at any level

Time

Thirty minutes

Handouts, Materials, and Equipment

- Paper and a pencil or pen for each participant
- One copy of *Empowered to Know Interview Suggestions* for each participant
- A flip chart and markers

Procedure

1. Tell the group that the typical employment interview contains questions such as: "Tell me about yourself." "What do you see yourself doing in five years?" or "What are your hobbies?" Explain that, although these questions can be effective, it is possible to enhance an interview with other questions and specific scenarios.

2. Distribute paper and pencils or pens. Ask each person to write, in a column down the left side of the paper, the following words: Who? What? Where? When? Why? How?

3. Ask the participants to call out empowering verbs that pertain to the interviewing process. Write their suggestions on the flip chart, such as: influence, affect, carry, obtain, impress, inspire, move, strike, sway, touch, model.

4. Have them use each word in the first column, add one of the verbs from the flip chart, and write a question that could be used for an interview. For instance: "*Who* influenced you to make your present career choice?" "*What* affected your decision to . . .?"

5. Now ask each of them to develop four or five sentence starters that interviewees can use pertaining to a specific position. For example: "If I had no limitations in this position, I would like to. . . ." "The first change I would make is. . . ." "The best way to . . . is to. . . ." Post some of their ideas on the flip chart.

6. Now ask participants to think of a problem that they have encountered in at least two different jobs they have held previously. (These scenarios should be open-ended and imply there are no right or wrong answers.) Have them develop questions that an interviewer could ask to find out about this type of problem.

7. Ask for volunteers to discuss how they would (or did) solve these problems. Have the group help to develop answers for questions about similar problems in the future.

8. Next, have the group list three options for closing the interview on a positive note, either as the interviewer or as the interviewee. At least one option should involve the decision not to hire the person or not to take a position if it is offered. Have the participants share their ideas with the group.

9. Give each participant a copy of *Empowered to Know Interview Suggestions* and go over the handout with them, giving examples of each item, taking suggestions from the group, and posting them on the flip chart.

Discussion

Discuss what participants have learned that they can use in the future, either when interviewing or being interviewed. Ask such questions as:

What have you been doing as an interviewer that may be having a negative effect? As an interviewee?

What have you been doing as an interviewer that has been successful in putting interviewees at ease and in gathering the maximum amount of pertinent information?

How can you incorporate the positive approach you discussed today the next time you interview someone? Are interviewed?

When is the best time of day for you personally to conduct an interview? For you to be interviewed?

How can you use empowering action words to develop questions or to think of answers beforehand?

What will you do differently in the future?

Source
Janice Kilgore

Empowered to Know Interview Suggestions

- Dare to be different, be positive!

- Go beyond what is on the resume or application. Seek what is not on the printed material. Look for what is between the lines on the resume. Touch the person's inner self by looking past his or her credentials.

- Avoid statements such as: "Give your five strengths and five weaknesses." Make every question or comment positive. Do not make the experience negative for the person by putting him or her on the defensive. Try to draw out the person's creativity and find the very best of his or her qualities.

- Do not engage in a power struggle. Make this a win-win situation.

- Bring out the best in people by posing statements and questions that cause them to describe meaningful experiences they have had. Help them to show you what they can do for your organization in an actual situation.

Group Interviewing Criteria

Objectives
- To help streamline the group interviewing process
- To give each member of the panel a sense of ownership
- To provide a cohesive and flexible group atmosphere
- To help panels evaluate applicants for the same position and achieve consensus

Uses
The activity is intended for training on how to conduct group interviews.

Time
Forty minutes

Audience
Primarily mid-management involved in employment interviewing

Handouts, Materials, and Equipment
- A pencil and paper for each participant

Procedure
1. Distribute paper and pencils to participants.
2. Ask each participant to write down five characteristics that a typical job applicant should possess, such as integrity, experience, etc.
3. Ask them to determine whether they personally possess these five characteristics and to revise their lists, if necessary.
4. Ask participants to form small groups of co-workers who actually interview applicants together (or any group for practice). Tell the groups to spend ten minutes consolidating their lists into criteria for employment with the company.

5. Have each group evaluate real or imaginary applicants by considering the extent to which they possess the employment criteria, using the following scale:

1-Very little or not at all

2-Somewhat

3-Moderately

4-Moderately high

5-Completely

Discussion

Use the following questions to wrap up the session and the learnings:

Were the outcomes of this activity realistic for an actual interview?

How could these procedures be used for an actual group interview?

Were the criteria you developed adequate? Too specific? Too general?

How quickly did the group reach consensus in determining the criteria? Why?

To what extent did participants feel a sense of ownership of the final result?

Did any one person dominate the process? How could this be changed?

Was this process more efficient than other, similar processes you have used? If so, in what ways?

Source
Janice Kilgore

More Than One Way to Skin a Question

Objectives

- To teach nonthreatening, indirect methods for finding specific information
- To practice asking open-ended questions
- To glean information through inductive methods

Uses

The activity is meant to teach an alternative method to direct questioning during an interview, when the person being interviewed may feel threatened or intimidated.

Audience

Any in any size group

Time

Thirty minutes

Handouts, Materials, and Equipment

- One set of *More Than One Way Information Sheets A* and *B* for each pair

Procedure

1. Divide the group into pairs. If the group is not even, you may join one pair or have one person serve as an observer.

2. Give *More Than One Way Information Sheet A* to one member of each pair and *More Than One Way Information Sheet B* to the other person, instructing them *not* to share what is on the sheets with one another.

3. Tell participants that they are to obtain the information listed on their sheets without asking for it directly. Give as an example that they may not ask someone directly whether he or she smokes, but might ask something such as "How do you feel about being in a room where other people are smoking?" Answer any procedural questions and have everyone begin with Sheet A.

4. Give each person using Sheet A ten minutes to obtain the information required and then switch and allow the other person ten minutes to obtain the information on Sheet B.

5. Bring everyone together for a general discussion.

Discussion

To help with discussion, ask the following questions:

Did you obtain all of the information required? Why or why not?

What kinds of information were easy to obtain? What kinds were more difficult to obtain?

What would you do differently the next time to obtain the information?

Give some examples of some indirect questions that you asked.

When would this technique be useful back on the job or in real life? How useful would it be?

Variation

You may want to make your own list of required information. The idea is not to make it too difficult and to let the participants have some fun while they are learning.

Source
Richard Whelan and Robert Merritt

More Than One Way Information Sheet A

Instructions: Obtain the information listed on this sheet without asking for it directly.

1. Mother's maiden name
2. Favorite type of music
3. Marital status
4. First car owned

More Than One Way Information Sheet B

Instructions: Obtain the information listed on this sheet without asking for it directly.

1. Date of birth
2. Last place of employment
3. Astrological sign
4. Name of first-grade teacher

Taking Charge

Objective

- To anticipate interviewer questions
- To help trainees learn tactics to deal with difficult questions
- To create a positive interviewing experience

Uses

The activity can be used to ready participants for any type of interviewing situation.

Time

Thirty to forty minutes

Handouts, Materials, and Equipment

- One copy of the *Taking Charge Interviewing Suggestions* for each participant
- Paper and a pencil for each participant
- A flip chart and markers

Procedure

1. Distribute the *Taking Charge Interviewing Suggestions*, paper, and a pencil to each participant. Give them time to read the list of suggestions.
2. Ask each participant to list ten action words to empower an interview, such as "experience," "question," "decision making," "energize," and "excitement."
3. Tell them to write each word in a sentence fragment that deflects a negative comment or question. They can do this by making it positive, using humor, using empowering words, or by taking the attitude that the one who is being interviewed is equally in charge of the outcome. List the following example on the flip chart for everyone to see:

Let me answer your question with a question: Where I would like to be in five years? I would like to be in a place much like yourself, a position of decision making, in order to utilize my skills in. . . .

4. After everyone has finished writing deflecting sentence fragments, have partici-pants divide into pairs. One person should serve as the interviewer and the other the interviewee.

5. Ask them to practice using their sentences in situations from their lives and then to switch roles. They should give one another feedback on their words and on the deflecting sentences, developing alternative statements if needed or desired.

Discussion

Wrap up the discussion with the following questions:

How might anticipation and preparation aid the interviewee?

Were you able to avert uncomfortable or negative situations by anticipating them and turning them into positive experiences?

Did you feel empowered by rephrasing questions to meet the interviewer's needs and then inserting your own experiences?

What other action words and sentences can you think of that could enhance your next interview experience?

Source
Janice Kilgore

Taking Charge Interviewing Suggestions

Instructions: Use this list of suggestions to prepare for any interview by empowering yourself. Remember that you have a role to play in the outcome, too. Some tried-and-true empowering sentences are:

Would you like me to tell you why I would be excellent in this job?

Allow me to tell you how I brought about that very thing in the past.

Instead of only one thing I can do to bring success to this position, let me tell you five things that will improve. . . .

For a more "gutsy" approach, do your homework on the needs of a company or what has been lacking in the position in the past. Provide solutions to solve problems, with the understanding that the company will give you the latitude to carry them out. Then say, "If I haven't accomplished these things in an agreed amount of time, replace me." This tactic is risky, but has worked many times.

Tri-Counseling

Objectives

- To explore counselor and client roles
- To experience a helping relationship from each point of view
- To learn how to help the client develop a system to solve problems

Uses

The activity is for teaching counseling techniques and the differences between counseling and interviewing.

Time

Sixty minutes

Audience

Any number of groups of three

Handouts, Materials, and Equipment

- One copy of the *Tri-Counseling Guidelines* for each participant
- One copy of the *Tri-Counseling Observer Form* for each participant
- Pencils or pens for each participant
- A flip chart and markers

Procedure

1. Have participants form groups of three and give each person one copy of the *Tri-Counseling Guidelines* and a pencil or pen.
2. Explain that each person will play the role of client, counselor, and observer one time. Go through the guidelines with participants, emphasizing that they are to talk about a real issue, not a fabricated one, when playing the client role.
3. Hand out observer forms and explain the role, noting that observers are not to participate during the session, but to observe and listen. After the session, they are to give feedback to the counselor only, not the client.

4. Have the triads begin, telling them they have five minutes for each counseling session, a total of three rounds for fifteen minutes. Walk around and encourage counselors to follow the guidelines and observers to fill in the observer forms. Warn participants when to change roles. Give a two-minute warning and then stop the sessions.

5. Allow observers five minutes to give feedback to the counselors (not the clients)— a total of fifteen minutes in three rounds. Encourage the observers to use what they have written on their observer forms as well as any other observations they may have. Keep track of the time and let participants know when to switch roles.

Discussion

After all rounds are complete, ask the group to discuss interviewing, counselor skills, relationships, trust, and awareness by addressing the following questions, posting salient points on a flip chart:

How did you feel about using real issues in the counseling sessions?

Which role was the most difficult to play? Why?

What general difficulties did you experience?

What differences can you see between counseling and interviewing?

What implications are there for someone who is interviewing someone else?

Would an effective interviewer necessarily be an effective counselor?

Source
Gary Wagenheim

Tri-Counseling Guidelines

Do
- Develop a trusting and helping relationship with the client
- Help the client solve his or her problem
- Help the client develop a system to solve future problems
- Help the client develop an awareness of the causes of problems

Do Not
- Give advice
- Give the answer
- Tell your own story
- Rush to achieve results

Getting Started
Get focused and center yourself before you start a session with a client. Be in touch with your own feelings and emotions. Take a few deep breaths and get ready to begin.

Engaging
Say hello. Face the client squarely and look him or her in the eye. Ask the client if he or she would like to talk about the issue. Start to work, but do not rush to an answer before you define the problem. Let the client set the pace. Be alert to what the client says to start the session, as it often is a clue to the problem. Be empathic and positive.

Being Specific
Help the client define the problem. Take the problem from the abstract to the specific by asking for details. Focus and clarify the problem by using active listening, e.g., "This is what I heard you say; is that what you meant?" Ask what the client is thinking when there are long silences. Encourage him or her with positive feedback such as head nods, leaning forward, and brief remarks. Do not be afraid of missing a point. If it is important, it will reoccur.

Generating Alternatives
Help the client develop alternatives by asking, "What are three options you can think of to solve your problem?" Help the client evaluate the options by weighing the costs and benefits. If he or she is stuck, ask, "If you had magical power to solve this problem and all the necessary resources, what would you do?"

Taking Action
Help the client develop a plan of action with specific dates. Use questions such as: "How is this problem going to be solved?" "What will be needed?" and "When will it be done?"

Closing
Set a date to check back with the client to see if the plan of action was implemented and the problem solved. At that time discuss any unfinished business.

Tri-Counseling Observer Form

Instructions: Silently observe the client–counselor interaction. Make notes below to enable you to give feedback to the counselor after the session.

What things did the counselor do that were effective?

What difficulties did the counselor experience?

What improvements could the counselor make in the future?

To what degree did the counselor follow the guidelines?

Other comments?

Leadership

Follow the Word Leader

Objectives

- To consider and evaluate important leadership behaviors
- To help participants integrate new knowledge
- To demonstrate the power of free association

Uses

Use this activity for training in leadership or creative thinking or for team building.

Audience

All levels in groups of four to seven

Time

Twenty to thirty minutes

Handouts, Materials, and Equipment

- Pens or pencils for each participant
- One set of stimulus word sheets for each group
- A flip chart and markers for each group

Procedure

1. *Prior to the workshop:* Write the following stimulus words at the top of separate sheets of paper, one word per sheet: power, authority, communication, behavior, results, teamwork, influence. Make one set for each group.

2. Explain that free association is a thinking process using one word as a stimulus to think of another word associated with it. Each successive word is then used as the stimulus for another. Give the example of "tree," which might stimulate the word "leaves," which might stimulate the word "table," and so on.

3. Have participants form groups of from four to seven members each. Distribute a set of stimulus word sheets and pencils to each group so that each person has a

different word from the others in his or her group. Give four sheets to a group with four people, five sheets to a group with five, and so on.

4. Ask participants to look at the stimulus word on their sheets of paper and generate two free associations for that word.

5. After everyone has completed this step, tell the participants to pass the sheets to the people on their right. Each person is then to free associate two more words using the last word on the list passed to them as a stimulus word.

6. Continue this process until each person in each group has contributed two associations for each sheet. Thus, if there are four people in a group, there should be 32 words on each sheet (4 people × 4 words × 2 associations = 32).

7. Give each group a flip chart and markers. Have each group select two words from each sheet and write them on the flip chart. Tell groups to discuss each word and strive for consensus on its implications for effective leadership. For instance, if one of the free associations for the word "power" is "strength," the group might conclude that effective leaders must demonstrate "the strength of their convictions" or "have the strength to deal with threats to the group."

8. If there is more than one group, ask each group to share all of its implications for leadership.

Discussion

Focus the discussion on what has been learned about leadership. Use the following questions to guide the group:

What were the major learnings your group had about leadership?

How does this approach to learning and discussion compare with more conventional lecture or group learning methods?

Are you likely to retain what you have learned longer? Why or why not?

Do you think that free association can help people think of more creative responses?

When else could it be used for clarifying a work situation?

Variation

If more time is available, have the groups discuss all of the free association words they wrote, rather than just two per sheet.

Source
Arthur VanGundy

It All Depends

Objectives

- To illustrate how leader effectiveness is determined by the situation
- To begin to evaluate one's own leadership style

Uses

Use the activity during management-development training or for a team-building session.

Audience

Managers or aspiring managers of equal status in groups of four to seven

Time

Forty-five to sixty minutes

Handouts, Materials, and Equipment

- One set per group of any set of toys or materials that can be assembled, such as TinkerToys®, Lincoln Logs®, Legos®, or any other wooden or plastic blocks
- One copy of the *It All Depends Theory Handout* for each participant
- Paper and pencils for each participant
- A flip chart and markers

Procedure

1. Divide participants into groups of four to seven. Tell them that they are going to participate in a leadership activity involving two different types of tasks:

   Task 1: Each group will build a bridge using the materials provided.

   Task 2: Each group will generate ideas for how to improve a bed.

2. Give each group enough materials to build a bridge and allow ten to fifteen minutes for completion.

3. Now hand out paper and pencils and ask the groups to generate lists of ways to improve a bed. After ten or fifteen minutes, have them stop and tell them to write down, individually, their reactions to the two tasks.

4. After a few minutes, tell them that they should pay particular attention to any differences in leadership behavior they observed in the group or about themselves.

5. After a few more minutes, ask participants to compare notes in their groups and to develop one list that all can agree with about the differences in leadership behavior between the two tasks.

6. Have each group report on its observations and post them on the flip chart.

Discussion

Lead a discussion of the emergent leadership styles for the two tasks. Ask whether they noticed a difference in their groups or whether the same person (or persons) was seen as the leader(s) for both tasks. If more than one person emerged as a leader for the same task in any groups, have them describe what happened and whether there was competition for the role.

Note that some group members may have contributed more than others. Ask the participants why they think this happened. (*Note:* Be prepared for someone to observe that no one emerged as a leader and that all members contributed equally. Although this is possible, such statements often reflect group norms of equality and team spirit.) Conclude by giving everyone a copy of the handout and discussing the points it makes.

Source
Arthur VanGundy

It All Depends Theory Handout

Research indicates that the nature of the task helps to determine various group behavior, especially leadership behavior. The first task required someone to decide what type of bridge to make and how to coordinate the efforts of group members. The second task, which was more abstract, required fewer coordinating behaviors and more facilitating behaviors.

Differences between tasks often determine who emerges as a leader within a group. Assuming that no appointed leader exists, the person most likely to influence others is the one (or two or three) perceived as best able to help the group perform its task.

In this case, a leader for the first task was likely to be someone proficient at coordinating the efforts of others and figuring out how to accomplish a sequence of activities. Because the second task was more open-ended without a definable product to produce, it required a different leadership style. Someone who excels at generating ideas, deferring judgment, and encouraging input of others will usually emerge as a leader for this type of task.

Sometimes two or more people will share the leadership role. Although their behaviors may not be identical, they should be complementary rather than competitive or they will impede the group process.

Some group members will contribute more than others, depending on the task also, although personality accounts for some differences. Some people may have difficulty observing leadership behavior when they are in the group themselves.

Leadership Inventory

Objectives

- To increase awareness of the characteristics of leadership
- To enhance group members' confidence in their leadership abilities

Uses

The activity can be used during leadership training for a work group, team, or board.

Audience

All levels of potential leaders

Time

Twenty to thirty minutes

Handouts, Materials, and Equipment

- One copy of the *Leadership Inventory* for each participant
- A pencil for each participant
- Masking tape
- A flip chart and markers

Procedure

1. Briefly discuss with the group the fact that leadership can come in many forms and that each member plays a unique role in the group. Have them list some of the roles they play in their work groups and post them on the flip chart.

2. Give each participant one copy of the *Leadership Inventory* and a pencil. Discuss the leadership characteristics listed on the worksheet so that everyone has the same definition of each.

3. Ask each participant to write his or her name on the worksheet and have someone use masking tape to put it on his or her back. (*Note:* Ideally, group members should wear informal clothing that would not be damaged from tape.)

4. After everyone has a copy of the *Leadership Inventory* on his or her back, have the participants mill around the room and place check marks next to leadership characteristics they believe that other people possess. Tell participants to check *at least one item* on every person's worksheet, but to be sure to check as many as apply to that person, even if someone else has already checked it. (*Note:* The number of checks will give participants an idea of their strengths.)

5. After everyone has checked qualities for everyone else, have participants remove their own sheets, be seated, and see what other group members perceive their leadership qualities to be.

Discussion

Lead a discussion of the experience, using the following questions as guides:

What surprises you most about how others perceive you?

Have you heard any of these perceptions before?

Do you feel that any of the perceptions are untrue? Could any be based on stereotypes or misconceptions?

If you filled out the *Leadership Inventory* for yourself, would it be similar or different from the composite group assessment? If different, in what way?

Do you feel that the assessment of your strengths and weaknesses is correct? Why or why not?

How are you similar or dissimilar from other group members? How does this benefit or hurt the group?

In what ways can you use your strengths to help the group attain its goals?

Source
Melinda M. Morris

Leadership Inventory

Your Name: _____

Instructions: Attach this *Leadership Inventory* to your back. Other group members will place a check next to any quality they perceive that you possess. Some qualities will have many check marks; others will not. Remember that successful groups include a variety of unique individuals who play different roles. This inventory will help you better understand your role in this group.

_____Creativity   _____Persistence

_____Ambition   _____Confidence

_____Strong Values   _____Calmness

_____Cleverness   _____Intelligence

_____Motivation   _____Intuition

_____Trustworthiness   _____Adaptability

_____Imagination   _____Likability

_____Empathy   _____Dedication

_____Sense of Humor   _____Tolerance

_____Open-Mindedness   _____Loyalty

There Must Be a Leader in This Group

Objectives

- To discover natural leaders within small groups
- To challenge a group to work as a team with or without a leader
- To explore unplanned teamwork

Uses

This activity helps to demonstrate key factors involved in productive leadership or can be used as an energizer or for a team-building session.

Audience

All levels

Time

Thirty to forty minutes

Handouts, Materials, and Equipment

- A good supply of 3″ × 5″ index cards or construction paper
- A supply of masking tape, string, and paper clips for each small group
- Scissors for each group
- A watch with a timer for the facilitator
- A flip chart and markers

Procedure

1. Divide participants into small groups and distribute materials to each group, including approximately twenty index cards or sheets of construction paper.
2. Tell them they are to build the tallest freestanding tower they can in a three-minute period with the materials they were given.

3. Tell them that the activity will start in two minutes. Look at your watch and *stop speaking*.

4. Answer any questions, but volunteer no further information. If asked, reinforce that they can only use the materials that they were given.

5. Tell the groups to begin and be sure to time them.

6. When three minutes are up, select the best tower.

Discussion

Ask them to discuss what happened and answer the following questions while you write the answers on the flip chart:

Did a leader emerge in any of the groups?

How were you able to construct towers if you did not have a leader?

What did not work well for the groups?

How could the project have worked better?

In what ways was this project like actual work on the job?

Variation

Groups can be asked to build something other than a tower, such as a box, a wagon, an airplane that must fly a set distance, or a sculpture that represents leadership and teamwork.

Source
Robert Alan Black

Listening

Been There, Said That

Objectives

- To experience the power of active listening
- To learn the importance of gathering high-quality information

Uses

The activity is useful for programs about dealing with criticism, exposing hidden agendas, and solving problems.

Audience

Any, in groups of three

Time

Fifteen minutes

Handouts, Materials, and Equipment

- A flip chart and markers

Procedure

1. Explain that this activity is designed to emphasize the importance of active listening.
2. Divide the group into trios and ask each group to designate its members as A, B, and C.
3. Ask person A in each group to think of three words that summarize an entire experience he or she has had, e.g., "I did that," "We went there," or "I learned something," but *not* to reveal the actual experience.
4. Instruct person B to learn what that experience was by reflecting back what person A says and then clarifying by asking Who? What? Where? When? or How? questions. Tell participants that person B is *not* allowed to guess, and person A is restricted to answering *only* the question that is asked.
5. Instruct person C in each group to observe the interaction and to intervene if B starts guessing or if A volunteers more information than is asked.

Discussion

Ask the group to describe what happened during the activity, giving examples of effective and ineffective listening and questioning. Conclude with a list of techniques on the flip chart for future use.

Variation

If time permits, use three rounds so that each person has an opportunity to practice effective listening and questioning skills.

Source
Rick Kirschner

Say What?

Objectives

- To demonstrate how listening barriers can interfere with effective communication
- To help participants become better listeners

Uses

The activity is very useful for communication training, especially when miscommunications have occurred, or for conflict management training.

Audience

Any level in pairs

Time

Twenty to thirty minutes

Handouts, Materials, and Equipment

- At least two sheets of paper and a pencil for each participant
- A flip chart and markers

Procedure

1. Have the participants divide into pairs, ideally with someone they do not know well. Hand out paper and a pencil to each person.

2. Tell everyone to write down, individually, five ways to make training sessions more fun. Give them a few minutes to think and write their answers.

3. Instruct the pairs to take turns reading their first ideas to one another, giving the following instruction aloud, using the exact wording: "Please comment on the other person's idea."

4. Have the pairs repeat this process, taking turns to hear one idea at a time and comment, until they have shared and commented on all of their ideas.

5. When every pair has finished, ask each person to write down, by memory only, (a) all the ideas that his or her partner had and (b) all of the comments that the partner made about his or her own ideas.

6. When participants have finished, have them compare their lists to see how well they did in recalling one another's ideas and comments.

7. Discuss the communication process that took place during this activity. In particular, ask the group to think of reasons, other than poor memory, why they may have had trouble recalling all of the information.

Discussion

Explain to the participants that two possible listening barriers are "prejudging" and "rehearsing." Prejudging occurs when we evaluate another person's ideas while listening to them; rehearsing occurs when we rehearse our own responses to what someone else is saying while he or she is still speaking.

Use the following questions as guides for discussion:

What were you thinking while your partner was talking?

How well did you listen to what your partner was saying?

How well did your partner listen to you?

To what extent were you judging the other person's ideas and comments?

To what extent were you rehearsing your comments or reactions to the other person's ideas or comments?

Did either of these thought processes interfere with your ability to remember what was said?

What other communication barriers might have prevented you from remembering as well as you might have?

Source
Arthur VanGundy

Talking Stick

Objectives

- To enhance group communication
- To create a format for uninterrupted disclosure rather than dialogue
- To emphasize listening skills as a necessary part of communication
- To debrief an important topic or close a workshop or seminar

Uses

This activity can be used as an icebreaker or as a closing to help participants integrate a learning experience. It helps to create group intimacy.

Audience

Any small group

Time

Fifteen to twenty minutes; allow at least one minute per person for each pass around the circle; more time is better

Handouts, Materials, and Equipment

- One "Talking Stick"

Procedure

1. *Prior to the workshop:* Find a wooden stick and paint or color it in some way. Attach beads and feathers or other decorations.
2. Invite the participants to sit in a circle. Join them, as an equal member of the circle. It is best if people sit on the ground or on the floor, but, if that is not possible, people also can sit in chairs.

3. Introduce the concept of the Talking Stick by saying:

The Talking Stick is used by Native Americans when elders meet to discuss important issues of the tribe. The stick is passed around a circle and used to facilitate communication by allowing each member present to have time to speak and be heard without being interrupted.

4. Explain that participants can only speak while they are holding the Talking Stick. Only one person can hold the stick and speak at any time. The rest of the group must listen and speak only when holding the Talking Stick. Explain the procedure by saying:

When you are holding the Talking Stick, you may speak. If you do not have it in your possession, please be silent and listen. The stick will be passed around the circle, and each member of the group will have a chance to share his or her comments or observations.

5. Describe the powerful nature of the Talking Stick and how it acts as a conduit to delve into people's essential facts and feelings:

The Talking Stick is a tool that possesses a certain power. Use that power to speak succinctly and wisely. Skip the details, the long winding stories about what happened to you on your way here, references to other people you know, or something someone once told you about this and that. Instead, go immediately to the core of what it is you want to say. Let the Talking Stick help you get right to the heart of the matter. Let it bring out your most salient thoughts and feelings.

6. Encourage people to focus on what the speaker is saying and not about how to respond. They should try to absorb and understand what is being said:

Do not think about what you are going to say when the Talking Stick comes around to you. Wait until the stick is in your hands. At that point, let it draw from you—in the moment—the information you have to tell the rest of the group.

7. Also give people permission not to talk when they have the stick:

If you have nothing to say, that is fine. The Talking Stick gives you an opportunity to speak, but it does not require you to say anything. Sometimes, if you have nothing to say, it is best to say nothing, but do hold the stick for a moment before you pass it on to see if any thoughts or ideas come to you.

8. Now that people know how to use the Talking Stick, begin by using the stick yourself to sum up the day's learnings for you (or whatever is an appropriate topic). Model the behavior you want from others. Keep your thoughts brief, to the point, and personal. Use "I" statements rather than "we" or "you." Hand the Talking Stick to someone next to you and then model good listening skills as you focus on what that individual has to say.

9. If time permits, allow the Talking Stick to pass around the circle at least twice. If time is short, use one pass around the circle and then place it in the center and encourage anyone who has more to add to take the stick, speak, and return it to the center.

10. Allow periods of silence for reflection and do not rush people to finish. The participants will pass the Talking Stick when they are finished. If they hold onto it for a moment, what they volunteer next might be very important. Remember, only the person holding the stick can speak and, unless someone is way off track or abuses the privilege, you must abide by the rules of the Talking Stick, too.

Discussion

In cohesive groups, people usually will share very thoughtful and personal information. With the Talking Stick and permission to speak uninterrupted, people often can speak their innermost feelings and thoughts. You should be able to detect if the group responds positively to this activity, but debrief afterward to see whether anyone felt uncomfortable and why. If there are people in the group who tend to monopolize group discussion, they may have had difficulty remaining silent. Discuss this with the group.

Variations

1. Introduce a subject for reflection at the beginning of the activity.

2. Begin by passing the stick and letting each individual talk about whatever comes to mind.

3. Use the stick to debrief a portion of the workshop or as a closing activity. It is often evident what the subject is, but it can be helpful to prompt people with a clue, such as "Let's use the Talking Stick to share what we can take away from this session," "Let's reflect on the major points we covered today and what we learned from this experience," or "What will you do differently as a result of what we covered today?"

4. A wand or baton or any other object can be used and passed as the Talking Stick, but it is a good idea to make a special stick or object to give it significance.

5. Each participant can be required to make his or her own Talking Stick to use to practice listening and speaking from the heart—or from the gut—when he or she is engaged in important conversations.

Source
Maggie Dugan

Will We or Won't We?

Objectives

- To demonstrate that how we say something has an impact on the message people receive
- To demonstrate how people interpret communication messages differently

Uses

Use this activity as an icebreaker to emphasize the importance of *how* things are said, to practice active-listening skills, and for general communication training.

Audience

Any

Time

Ten minutes

Handouts, Materials, and Equipment

- One copy of *Will We or Won't We Have a Meeting Today* for each participant
- One copy of the *Will We or Won't We Have a Meeting Today Facilitator's Guide* for the trainer
- A pencil for each participant
- A flip chart and markers

Procedure

1. Explain to participants that they will take a listening test during which they will hear a sentence read six different times. Each time it is read, they are to decide what the sentence means and put the sentence number in the blank provided.
2. Distribute one copy of *Will We or Won't We Have a Meeting Today* and a pencil to each participant.
3. Using the *Will We or Won't We Have a Meeting Today Facilitator's Guide*, read each statement in the order given, emphasizing the highlighted word in each case.

4. After you have read each sentence, tell participants the sentence number so that they can write it in the blank corresponding to the meaning.

5. After you have read the statement all six ways, ask the participants to identify the correct responses. List the correct answers as they give them, from top to bottom, on a flip chart.

Discussion

Discuss how important it is to listen for meaning. Ask for ways that simple misinterpretations of what others say can affect their daily communications. Point out examples from your own experience with the group, if possible, and ask for their own examples. Urge them to practice their listening skills.

Source
Peter R. Garber

Will We or Won't We Have a Meeting Today

_____ Statement of fact indicating that there will be no meeting today.

_____ Statement indicating that there will be something other than a meeting today.

_____ Statement indicating that someone else will be attending a meeting today.

_____ Statement that there definitely will not be a meeting today.

_____ Statement indicating that there will be more than one meeting today.

_____ Statement indicating that there will be a meeting, but not today.

Will We or Won't We Have a Meeting Today Facilitator's Guide

Instructions: Read each statement below in a normal voice, as indicated in the instructions.

1. Statement indicating that there will be a meeting, but not today.

   Emphasize the word *today.* Say: "We will not have a meeting *today.*"

2. Statement indicating that there will be something other than a meeting today.

   Emphasize the word *meeting.* Say: "We will not have a *meeting* today."

3. Statement of fact indicating that there will be no meeting today.

   Simply read the statement with no particular emphasis on any word. Say: "We will not have a meeting today."

4. Statement indicating that there will be more than one meeting today.

   Emphasize the word *a.* Say: "We will not have *a* meeting today."

5. Statement that there definitely will not be a meeting today.

   Emphasize the word *not.* Say: "We will *not* have a meeting today."

6. Statement indicating that someone else will be attending a meeting today.

   Emphasize the word *we.* Say: "*We* will not have a meeting today."

Answers: 3, 2, 6, 5, 4, 1

Negotiation

How to Win Over the Boss

Objective

- To prepare employees to present an advocacy message to a supervisor

Uses

The activity is helpful for teaching negotiation skills and persuasive communication techniques or for general employee training.

Audience

All levels

Time

Thirty minutes for preparation and discussion and five or six minutes per presentation

Handouts, Materials, and Equipment

- One copy of the *How to Win Over the Boss Advocacy Guidelines* for each participant
- One copy of the *How to Win Over the Boss Scenario* for each participant

Procedure

1. Briefly present the concept of advocacy by reading the following to the group:

   All effective communication is tailored to a specific audience. A boss is no different. Advocacy is the principal skill involved in "managing" your supervisor. That is, in order to effectively persuade your boss, you should follow advocacy guidelines.

2. Distribute copies of the *How to Win Over the Boss Advocacy Guidelines* (or present them on an overhead) and ask the group to read along with you while you read them aloud.

3. Divide the participants into small groups of four to six people and give each participant a copy of the *How to Win Over the Boss Scenario*.

4. Instruct the groups to prepare and present a persuasive message to "the boss" based on the scenario, using the advocacy strategies. Give them about ten minutes for preparation.

5. Have each group present its argument for the large group, then lead a wrap-up discussion.

Discussion

Bring participants back from their individual arguments to the general principles of advocacy and how they can use them in the future. Use the following questions to focus the discussion:

What role do advocacy strategies play in the negotiation process?

How might these strategies help you negotiate a deal?

What creative strategies emerged in your group from these advocacy messages?

In what ways did group members gear their messages specifically to the boss?

Why is analyzing the supervisor's preferences important?

Which advocacy message was the most persuasive? Why?

Source
Merry C. Buchanan

How to Win Over the Boss Advocacy Guidelines

Instructions: Use the following guidelines to communicate with and influence your supervisor more effectively.

Plan your strategy carefully.

Explain why your supervisor should listen to what you have to say.

Gear the argument to your boss's styles of learning and listening.

Assess your boss's technical knowledge.

Garner support from others.

Cultivate your communication skills.

How to Win Over the Boss Scenario

Situation: The members of your group report to a boss who is dogmatic and practical, but does not express himself or herself often. In fact, your boss is not at all expressive and it is difficult to tell how he or she feels about you or your work.

You and your co-workers would like to receive, and feel that you deserve, recognition for quality work. As a group, you do not necessarily seek monetary rewards, but would like other types of recognition for a job well done.

Devise an advocacy message that will focus on your boss's preferences and needs and yet still will achieve your goals as a group.

Lobbying

Objectives

- To develop a grassroots lobbying team or any presentation team
- To simulate lobbying before elected officials or regulators
- To demonstrate how to influence elected officials
- To demonstrate democracy at work

Uses

The activity can be used during a team-building session to show the powerful effects of personal contact or to prepare a group for a lobbying effort.

Audience

Inexperienced groups of twelve to forty who want to learn how to lobby for a position, including elected officials and the media

Time

Ninety to one hundred twenty minutes

Handouts, Materials, and Equipment

- One copy of the *Lobbying Role-Play Rules* for each participant
- One copy of the *Lobbying Community Background Sheet* for each participant
- The appropriate instruction sheets for role players
- Name tags and pens or markers
- A flip chart and markers

Procedure

1. Inform the participants that they will be taking part in a simulated lobbying experience. Give everyone copies of the *Lobbying Role-Play Rules* and read them aloud.
2. Answer any questions and have the group "elect" an official member of the State Senate (or Congress or the City Council). Put a name tag on the elected official that says "Landslide."

3. Ask "Landslide" to select a legislative aide or staff assistant and put a name tag on that person saying "Crusty."

4. Assign the remaining participants to one of three groups: Business, Labor, or Environmental, as follows:

   Business: Business Lobbyist 1, Business Lobbyist 2, Business Lobbyist 3, etc.

   Labor: Labor Lobbyist 1, Labor Lobbyist 2, Labor Lobbyist 3, etc.

   Environmental: Environmental Lobbyist 1, Environmental Lobbyist 2, Environmental Lobbyist 3, etc.

   Put name tags on people that indicate their roles. Additional participants should be assigned equally to the three groups and labeled as Business Lobbyist 4, Labor Lobbyist 4, and Environmental Lobbyist 4, etc.

5. Have participants form groups according to role and give each person a copy of the *Lobbying Community Background Sheet* and the appropriate role instruction sheet. Tell them that they have ten minutes to read the sheets and their instructions, design a group strategy, and initiate their first contacts.

6. After they have made their first contact, give the additional instruction sheets to Labor and Environment.

7. After ten minutes, announce that the final vote will be in twenty minutes. Periodically call out the time remaining to build tension.

8. Announce when the time is up and tell Landslide that he or she must vote now. Ask for his or her decision and why the decision was made. Then lead a wrap-up discussion of the activity.

Discussion

This is a fun role play and the debriefing may stimulate a great many comments. Note on the flip chart what influenced Landslide's vote positively and what influenced it negatively. Ask him or her to describe how it felt when others were trying to influence the vote.

Ask the participants what they tried, what worked, what did not work, and why. Point out the impact of trying to bribe an official or threatening retaliation. Ask for examples of the many possible "correct" points of view and corroborating data. Bring out the importance of forging coalitions, working with the senator's staff, and communicating early and often. Point out how long it takes to develop a position and yet how short the time may be before a vote is taken. Participants should also see that the background of an elected official makes a world of difference.

Variation

After the simulation has been run once, try using the group's real issues for another simulation. This time predict the opposition's likely lobbying positions and tactics. (*Note:* It is generally best to practice first to show the principles of lobbying before participants become emotionally involved in their own causes.)

Source
Kip L. Lilly

Lobbying Role-Play Rules

Objectives

The objectives of the role play are for each group (business, labor, or environmental) to convince the state senator, Landslide, to vote for the environmental bill most favorable to its position during the first round of voting.

Rules

1. Each group may contact the senator's office staff or the representative only the number of times listed on its instruction sheet.

2. Any direct verbal communication is considered to be a contact.

3. Contacts with the senator *must* go through the senator's legislative aide, Crusty.

4. No contact can last more than *two* minutes. Taking more than two minutes will result in an automatic vote against your position.

5. Each lobbying group will have ten minutes to read the material and discuss and agree on its position before determining a lobbying strategy.

6. You must follow these instructions and any additional instructions that group members may receive. Be sure that you understand these rules well before you begin, as the facilitator will not answer any questions during the role play.

Lobbying Community Background Sheet

Political Situation

The Fifth District of the state of Superior recently elected a new moderate senator, A. Landslide Official, by a scant 2 percent of votes, 51 percent to 49 percent, in a district evenly divided among Democrats, Republicans, and Independents.

Landslide has hired an old-time political pro, Crusty Staffer, to serve as his legislative assistant and head his office staff. Landslide heavily relies on Crusty's experience and opinions. Crusty, loyal but unfamiliar with the Fifth District, guards Landslide's time closely and actively protects him from "outside" pressure groups unknown to him (Crusty) and with whom Landslide has not previously met.

The first vote before the senate this term is on three different environmental bills. One bill is very complicated and controversial, designed to clean up the environment. The others represent more moderate proposals. It looks as if the vote will be close, and the three groups that will be most affected by the proposed legislation are attempting to influence every vote: the environmental lobby, the labor lobby, and the business lobby.

The Proposed Legislation

If passed, the first bill, SS.1, would establish a new state cabinet office, the Department of Clean Air, Recycling, and Environment (DO-CARE). DO-CARE would have strict control over all aspects of ambient air quality, telling businesspeople where they could locate new plants, what kind of pollution-control devices they would have to use, and when they had to install pollution-control devices. The new department would be advised by a board of five policy-setting commissioners, including two trade unionists, two environmental spokespeople, and one person with either an engineering or business background.

The second bill up for consideration, SS.2, would continue current trends, leaving responsibility for the environment with the Superior Environmental Protection Agency (SEPA). However, it would give SEPA subpoena powers to determine basic manufacturing and engineering processes, to shut down new plant construction, and to cut off all local, state, and federal funds or bonds for any project that did not meet SEPA's Clean Air Standards and Evaluation (SEPA-CASE).

The third bill, SS.3, would divide clean air responsibilities. The Department of Health and Welfare (HAW) and SEPA would set standards for ambient air quality based on cost/benefit analysis and known health standards for toxicity. They would also devise programs for retraining and relocating employees working in industries that were closed or substantially altered to meet clean air standards.

The Department of Commerce and Economic Development and Opportunity (DO-CEDO) would be responsible for establishing performance standards to reduce or abate pollution. DO-CEDO would be charged with doing away with design standards wherever possible. DO-CEDO would also offer tax incentives to industries that improved both ambient air quality and productivity.

Lobbying Instructions for Landslide

Instructions: You are A. Landslide Official, a newly elected member of the Superior State Senate from the Fifth District. You must decide which proposed clean air legislation described in the handout to vote for.

Your Role

1. Read the *Lobbying Community Background Sheet* first, but decide how to vote based on the arguments and lobbyist pressures presented and the advice of your legislative aide, Crusty Staffer.

2. At the end, when you vote, be prepared to tell the whole group your decision and to take one minute to explain why you voted as you did.

Additional Instructions for Landslide

Instructions: Vote based on the presentations and your *own values and conscience,* after briefly consulting with Crusty Staffer.

Lobbying Instructions for Crusty Staffer

Instructions: You are a legislative aide to A. Landslide Official, a newly elected member of the Superior State Senate from the Fifth District. You have a great deal of experience as a legislative aide, but have not known Landslide long and are not familiar with the Fifth District.

Your Role

1. Your job is to protect your boss, A. Landslide Official, from lobbyists.
2. Deny each group access to the senator during its initial visit.
3. After that, be tough on the groups, but be fair in giving them access to the senator.
4. Advise the senator of the time just before the vote will be taken.
5. Have a good time with your role.

Additional Instructions for Crusty Staffer

Instructions: Although you are to deny access to each group on its first try, *DO allow any coalition groups to see Landslide.*

Lobbying Instructions for Environmental Lobbyists

Instructions: You represent environmental interests trying to convince A. Landslide Official to vote for the bill most favorable to the environment, SS.1.

Your Role

1. You will have *four* opportunities to contact Senator A. Landslide Official.

2. Any one of you can speak for your cause. In fact, the more, the merrier. Select a principal spokesperson, Forrest Green, and indicate his or her position by a name tag.

3. Later, you will receive a thought-gram from the Coalition to Protect and Save Most Everything. You may choose to follow its suggestions or not, as your collective individual consciences dictate. However, you should be aware that, in the past, the Coalition has won big victories using the types of techniques they may suggest.

4. You have ten minutes to determine your position and strategy and to make contact with the senator.

Lobbying Instructions for Labor Lobbyists

Instructions: You are a labor lobbyist who will attempt to convince Senator A. Landslide Official to vote for the environmental bill more favorable to your position.

Your Role

1. You will have *three* opportunities to contact Senator A. Landslide Official.

2. You must choose a spokesperson, Strike Organizer. *Only he or she can speak for the labor delegation.* Use a name tag to identify this person.

3. Expect a fax message from International Union Headquarters. You *must* comply with what it says.

4. You have ten minutes to determine your strategy and make a first contact.

Lobbying Instructions for Business Lobbyists

Instructions: You are a business lobbyist who will attempt to convince Senator A. Landslide Official to vote for the environmental bill more favorable to your position.

Your Role

1. Your group will have *two* contact opportunities with Senator A. Landslide Official.

2. Choose a spokesperson, Phineas Phogbound, for your delegation. Identify that person with a name tag. However, any one of you may speak for business or his or her personal point of view.

3. You have ten minutes to determine your strategy and make a first contact.

INTERNATIONAL UNION HEADQUARTERS
6250 Arbitration Drive
Labor Line, MI 98765

FAX

To: Strike, president, Local 123
From: George Menace, president, International Generic Trades

Alright, you brothers and sisters in the union. Here's your instructions:
Send in LOTS of cards and letters. I mean . . . bury 'em!

THOUGHT-GRAM |||➤

Coalition to Protect and Save Most Everything
6666 Peaceful Meadow Lane
Aesthetic, CA 96767

To: Environmental Lobby
From: Tippi Treebough

    Congratulations on your courageous stand! We
at the Coalition applaud your efforts and stand
united with you.
    As a thought, you might try staging a
demonstration and inviting the media to help
educate the legislators about our cause. By the
way, do you have a slogan that can be chanted?
    You might also start a grassroots letter-
writing campaign or publish a list of the "Clean"
and "Dirty" legislators.

Yours faithfully in saving most everything,

Tippi

More Similar Than Different

Objectives

- To understand and identify barriers to negotiation
- To explore the role of stereotypes as obstacles to open negotiation

Uses

Use this activity when stereotypes and negative perceptions hamper negotiation, when participants seek to identify common ground, or to encourage more open communication. It can be used for general employee training, especially for sales and customer service representatives.

Audience

All levels

Time

Forty-five to sixty minutes

Handouts, Materials, and Equipment

- A flip chart and felt-tipped markers or whiteboard and markers

Procedure

1. Have each participant think of an individual or group who is opposed to them in some way, such as labor/management, sales staff/customers, other work groups in the organization, etc.

2. Ask the participants to call out words or characteristics that describe the group or individual they have identified while you write the words in a column on the far left side of the flip chart.

3. Now instruct the participants to call out words or characteristics that they think the opposition group or individual would use to describe them (the participants). Write these words in a column down the far right side of the flip chart.

4. Ask the participants to identify words or characteristics in either list that are stereotypes. Cross these words off each list as they are mentioned.

5. Have the participants call out words or characteristics that are common to both groups. These may be common goals, ideas, attitudes, demographics, values, or beliefs. Write the words in a column between the other two lists in the middle of the flip chart.

Discussion

Find out what participants have learned by asking the following questions:

What did you learn from this activity?

How might stereotypes act as barriers to open communication?

Do you try to avoid stereotypes when you communicate with the opposition group? Why or why not?

How could you use the characteristics that both groups have in common to begin an open dialogue?

Which list of characteristics plays the largest role in your negotiation with the other group? Why?

How might you overcome differences between yourself and others?

Do you usually acknowledge real differences between yourself and others? Should differences be discussed? Why or why not?

Do you feel you are more similar to than different from the other group? Why or why not? Did you feel that way before this activity?

How will what you have learned help your negotiation with the other group? Can you see them as partners in the negotiation process rather than as adversaries?

Variation

This activity may be used as a diversity activity to discuss similarities, differences, and stereotypes of any racial, ethnic, or gender groups.

Source
Melinda M. Morris

Saucy Deal

Objectives

- To increase awareness of the variables involved in negotiating an agreement
- To enhance negotiation skills
- To demonstrate how difficult the negotiation process can be

Uses

This activity can be used when ineffective negotiation skills hamper employee productivity or for general training of new managers or anyone who must use negotiation skills on a regular basis.

Audience

All levels, but especially management and sales employees, in groups of five

Time

Forty-five to sixty minutes

Handouts, Materials, and Equipment

- One copy of the *Saucy Deal Background Information* for each participant
- A paper and pencil for each observer
- A flip chart and markers

Procedure

1. Give one copy of the *Saucy Deal Background Information* to each participant and ask people to read the sheets. Give them time to do this.
2. Divide participants into groups of five, then have each group subdivide into two dyads, each containing two Sams or Samanthas and two Tonys or Tonis.
3. Instruct the fifth person in each group to serve as an observer to note the negotiation process used by each side and any unique incidents that occur.
4. Tell participants that they will have twenty minutes to negotiate a deal based on the information provided.

5. After twenty minutes, ask the observers to provide feedback to the dyads regarding the negotiations and the final agreements. Encourage the dyads to ask questions and discuss the activity with one another and the observer.

6. After about five to ten minutes of discussion, ask each group to give a brief presentation to the total group on the deal that was negotiated and the conclusions they have drawn about the activity. Post pertinent comments on a flip chart.

Discussion

Use the following questions to wrap up the discussion:

What general negotiation processes and principles did you use during the activity?

How did you reconcile long- versus short-term considerations?

What seemed to be the most difficult issues to resolve? The easiest?

What marketing problems might the merger create?

How did you deal with investment requirements, profit issues, participation, and scope of the business (e.g., keeping the pasta business)?

What management problems might be created by some of the solutions?

What effect might the reputation of a store have on a merger?

What, if any, problems were created by buy-out offers?

In what ways did dyads differ in their negotiation processes and outcomes? Why were there differences?

What would you do differently if you were to start over?

What effect did using dyads have on the outcome? What would have been different if only one person had done the negotiating?

Variation

Have participants modify the background information or make up their own scenarios. If possible, use an actual negotiation situation with which someone was involved.

Source
Bill Lazarus and Arthur VanGundy

Saucy Deal Background Information

Sam's Pizza is a well-established parlor that makes the best pizza on the west side of town. Tony's Pizza has three stores that reign supreme on the south side. Sam, 58, also has a wholesale pasta business and makes a special type of ravioli for the best restaurants in town. Unfortunately, this phase of Sam's business barely breaks even. Sam, however, believes that by sticking with it, it will eventually make a lot of money. Sam's child, Kid-O'-Sam, expects to receive a big slice of the business when Sam retires. Sam is known for making the best sauce and toppings in the state. Tony, 31, however, rolls out the best crust in the state.

Sam has cash in the bank and a solid line of credit as well as excellent vendor relations and a good reputation. Tony has received an offer to establish three more stores in town. However, Tony is cash poor and does not have much business experience.

A merger makes sense to both Sam and Tony, but how to accomplish it is a real toss up. Tony is not very fired up about the pasta business, and the two cannot agree on what to call a joint venture. They also have cooked up a list of other questions such as: How will decisions be made? How will it be run? How will profits be split?

The basic question for each dyad to negotiate is: Should Tony let Sam buy out Tony's Pizza? If so, what will be the terms of the deal, answering the questions above and any others that come up.

Problem Solving

I Never Thought of It That Way!

Objectives

- To take a broader view of problems and their solutions in order to enhance creativity
- To illustrate that our thought processes can be inhibited by patterned thinking

Uses

Use this activity to demonstrate how easy it is to respond quickly to an idea or concept based on "old" patterns of thought, which can result in missed opportunities and miscommunications.

Audience

All levels, individually or in any size group

Time

Fifteen minutes

Handouts, Materials, and Equipment

- One copy of the *I Never Thought of It That Way! Questions* for the facilitator

Procedure

1. Ask the group to listen carefully as you read the questions from the *I Never Thought of It That Way! Questions* sheet. Read quickly, while remaining understandable. Read one question at a time and ask for an answer.

2. Share the "standard" answers to the questions: 1 = seven, 2 = eleven, 3 = the match, 4 = they were not playing one another.

3. Ask the group if they can think of any other answers for any of the questions, for instance: 1 = any number were on the right, so any number were on the left; 2 = none, as the ancient Mayans used a calendar divided into eighteen months of twenty days each; 3 = the room, with the match being lit implied; 4 = they played more than five games. (*Note:* The problem says they played five games without a draw, but they also could have played a sixth game with each winning three.) The group's ability to discover alternative answers will improve with each succeeding question.

Discussion

Discuss why it took time, at first, to discover the "right" answers. Look for people to say that we are conditioned to listen and respond in prescribed ways that we do not even realize. Then ask the following questions:

What ways can we use to break the paradigm of patterned thinking?

When would you like to be able to practice thinking in a new way?

Why does it become easier to answer each question as you go through them?

Variation

Divide the group into teams and allow five minutes for solving the puzzles. Award prizes to the group with the most correct answers.

Source
Leslie Berger and Nance Guilmartin

I Never Thought of It That Way! Questions

Question One

A farmer had eighteen pigs and all but seven died. How many were left?

Question Two

Some months, such as October, have thirty-one days. Only February has twenty-eight, except in leap year when it has twenty-nine days. How many months have thirty days?

Question Three

If you only had one match and entered a cold, dimly lit room where there was a kerosene lamp, an oil heater, and a wood-burning stove, which would you light first?

Question Four

Two women play checkers. They play five games without a draw game, and each woman wins the same number of games. How can this be?

Pipe Cleaner Challenge

Objectives

- To demonstrate that most of us make assumptions about problems automatically, accept instructions without question, follow directions as given, and play by the rules
- To encourage participants to challenge assumptions, question instructions, ignore directions, and break rules when confronted with a problem or opportunity

Uses

The activity is ideal for illustrating how to stimulate creative thinking, expression, and problem solving.

Audience

Any level in any size group

Time

Thirty minutes

Handouts, Materials, and Equipment

- Ten pipe cleaners per participant
- A flip chart and markers

Procedure

1. Introduce the activity as a creativity challenge. Give ten pipe cleaners to each participant.
2. Say: "Make a hat out of five pipe cleaners." Do not elaborate beyond that simple instruction. If anyone asks a question at this point, simply repeat the statement: "Make a hat out of five pipe cleaners."
3. Allow participants approximately ten minutes to complete the task.

4. Review the results. Point out several of the hats and comment on their uniqueness. Compliment the group on how well they met the challenge of making a hat out of pipe cleaners. (*Note:* 99 percent of all participants who complete this activity will make a hat using only five pipe cleaners, as instructed.)

5. Point out to the group that everyone worked entirely alone without speaking to anyone else to make a hat for a human's head using only five pipe cleaners. Discuss why they all followed what they assumed to be the "rules" of the activity.

6. Write "Challenge Assumptions" and "Break Rules" on the flip chart. Ask participants how they might have challenged assumptions or broken the rules when making their pipe-cleaner hats. Record their responses on the flip chart. (*Note:* Some examples to look for include: "worked in teams," "used more pipe cleaners," "made something other than a hat," "moved to a different part of the room to work," etc.).

7. Instruct the participants to take their remaining five pipe cleaners and to make another hat, but to do so in a way that challenges assumptions and/or breaks the rules. Allow participants ten minutes to make their hats.

Discussion

Review the results, asking participants to describe their creations and to point out how they challenged an assumption or broke the rules in completing this task. Have them compare their results. Then ask the following questions:

Which time was more satisfying, enjoyable, or rewarding? Why was that?

Is there a specific problem or opportunity that you have now at work? How could you use the technique you have learned to solve the problem?

Source
Don Crane

Problem as Solution to Another Problem

Objectives

- To help think about a problem in a new way
- To help define a problem so that it can be solved more easily
- To come up with innovative solutions to problems

Uses

If many different possible solutions to a problem have been tried with little success, this activity is useful because sometimes the way we think about a problem keeps us stuck in it.

Audience

Anyone interested in solving problems, but especially managers or strategic planners or people in authority who are looking for innovative and visionary solutions to a problem

Time

Thirty to sixty minutes

Handouts, Materials, and Equipment

- Paper and pencils for participants

Procedure

1. Distribute paper and pencils and instruct participants to think of a problem that seems unsolvable and to write it down in one sentence.

2. Ask, "How could your problem be a solution to another problem?" Provide examples, such as:

"Eating too much" as a solution to boredom or frustration.

"Team conflict" as a solution to a lack of awareness of job responsibilities and purpose.

"Vandalism" as a solution to lack of customer service and sense of injustice.

"Catching a cold" as a solution to needing time to rest.

Tell them to write down as many ways as possible that their problem could be used to solve another problem, thinking as creatively as they can so that new insights and perspectives can occur.

3. Next, have the participants use their lists as stimuli to find solutions to their original problems. Again, they should list as many ideas as possible, however unlikely, in order to stir creativity.

Discussion

Check with participants for especially creative solutions they would like to share with the group. Discuss the implications of this method for solving problems on the job.

Source
Judith Morgan and Andre de Zanger

Things That Rhyme

Objectives

- To demonstrate how patterns can mislead us to believe that something is correct or appropriate when it may not be
- To help move out of a problem "rut" and view problems from a different perspective

Uses

The activity helps to change conventional thinking about a problem. It can also be used as an icebreaker or as part of a communication-training program.

Audience

Any group of two or more

Time

Five minutes

Handouts, Materials, and Equipment

- One copy of the *Things That Rhyme Facilitator's Guide*

Procedure

1. Tell participants that you will give them a series of questions to answer. They are to answer each question in unison, repeating the answer three times together.
2. Using the *Things That Rhyme Facilitator's Guide*, read the first question and give the participants the answer so that they can practice answering three times in unison.
3. Now read the next three questions, pausing for them to answer each one three times in unison.
4. The group will incorrectly answer the last question as "yoke" rather than "albumen." Ask them to think about their answer again.

Discussion

Ask the group why they gave the wrong answer to such a simple question. They probably will respond that it rhymed or fit a pattern with their other answers and that the others said the same thing. Discuss why we should avoid assuming something is correct just because it seems to fit a pattern or because someone else says it. Have them list possible learnings for their own work lives.

Source
Peter R. Garber

Things That Rhyme Facilitator's Guide

Instructions: Read each sentence clearly. Tell participants to answer each question as a group, repeating the answer in unison three times. Have them practice responding in unison on the first question.

1. A funny story with a punch line is called a _____. *(answer = joke)*

2. When you are thirsty you buy a can of _____. *(answer = Coke™)*

3. You tie things down with a _____. *(answer = rope)*

4. The white of the egg is called the _____. *(answer = albumen)*

Whole-Brain Writing

Objectives

- To emphasize that creative problem solving involves both left- and right-brain thinking
- To practice defining problems and generating ideas
- To determine if additional problem analysis improves idea generation

Uses

Use the activity to define problems and to train people in creative problem-solving methods.

Audience

Individuals or groups at any level

Time

Thirty to forty minutes

Handouts, Materials, and Equipment

- Paper and a pencil for each participant
- A flip chart and markers

Procedure

1. Discuss standard theories about creative thinking originating in the right brain, with the left brain being more linear and analytical. Have the group select an open-ended problem they are actually experiencing that requires creative solutions, i.e., right-brain thinking, but state that they will begin with a typical left-brain problem-solving method.

2. Post the following instructions on the flip chart:

   Develop a one-sentence statement of the problem.

   Identify three major points (e.g., reactions, data) about this problem.

   Expand on each point by writing for at least one minute.

3. Keep track of the time and stop everyone from writing after ten minutes.

4. Now tell participants that they will find even more solutions to the problem by shifting from left-brain to right-brain thinking. Tell them to form pairs and brainstorm more possible solutions by reading over what each of them wrote earlier and thinking of every possible solution without trying to judge it in any way.

Discussion

Discuss the activity by using the following questions:

How did this experience compare with other brainstorming sessions in which you have participated?

How did developing a one-sentence problem statement affect your idea generation?

What, if any, effect did identifying three major points about the problem have on your ability to generate new ideas? Do you think it helped you generate more ideas or held you back?

Did the move from analytical problem solving to creative brainstorming help spur your idea generation? Why or why not?

Was it helpful to apply both types of thinking to the same problem? Were the results superior to what they might have been with only one method?

Source
Margaret J. King and Arthur VanGundy

Team Building

Composition

Objectives

- To provide a cohesive environment, leading to harmonious thinking and exploration
- To reach a level of nonverbal communication that goes beyond typical experiences
- To learn to employ these practices for work-related tasks

Uses

Use the activity when group morale is low or when a group needs to learn how to work together better.

Audience

All levels in groups of four to six

Time

Thirty minutes

Handouts, Materials, and Equipment

- A sheet of 11″ × 17″ paper and a pencil for each group
- A collection of common objects found in an office, such as a pencil sharpener, chair, pen, or stapler, with at least one for each participant

Procedure

1. Define "music" as any combination of sounds and silences that, when combined, make a musical work.
2. Instruct the participants to select one object from the materials to use as a musical instrument and then to form groups of four to six members each.
3. When participants are settled, tell them to avoid thinking of an object's intended use, but to think of *three* ways that it can be used to make *different* musical sounds.

4. Help people with the following example, if necessary:

The three unique sounds can be soft, medium, and loud. This involves finding a series of musical textures, known as timbre (pronounced tamber). For instance, a ballpoint pen might make sounds in several ways: pumping up and down on the end to extend the point results in a clicking sound (soft); running the clip across the edge of a table makes a percussive sound (medium); and tapping the pen on the side of a table makes a loud sound.

5. Give sheets of paper and pencils to each group and tell each group to choose a recorder. They are to establish a system of notation unique to their group's composition and record a composition that they will play for the large group. Nontraditional symbols could include symbolic recognition and performance (e.g., # = tap or soft, * = shake or medium, and ~ = strike or loud). These symbols may include variations of loudness and softness (dynamics) and speed, as well as timbre.

6. Have each group extemporaneously compose a piece and record it, using its notation system. Give everyone time to compose and record their pieces.

7. When they are finished, give the groups a few minutes to practice playing their compositions and then have them take turns performing for the large group.

Discussion

Discuss the experience with participants, using some of the following questions to bring out what was learned:

Did you experience any problems in creating your musical works?

How did you decide which symbols to use to record your composition? Was any negotiation necessary? Was a consensus reached, or did some people decide on their own? What does this indicate about how your group operates?

Did the compositions communicate anything about the groups at a more sensory, nonverbal level? How can this type of communication be used on the job? How can feelings be incorporated into job-related tasks?

What type of group climate existed during the performance? What unique characteristics did you possess as a group at that moment that made the experience memorable?

Variations

1. Use inexpensive rhythm instruments, such as hand drums, tambourines, bells, castanets, wooden blocks, or claves, which can be purchased from teacher stores and educational supply houses.

2. Have one or more participants "conduct" the groups to bring out the interpretation while cuing participants.

3. Have completely improvisational performances without recording the compositions in advance, playing solely what a "conductor" dictates, according to the dynamics, tempo, shape of piece, and mood.

Source
Janice Kilgore

Excuuuse Me!

Objectives

- To destroy the "obstacle course" of excuses that impedes teamwork
- To illustrate how excuses can reduce team cohesion

Uses

Use the activity for team building, quality improvement, cross-training, or implementing ideas.

Audience

Self-managed teams, team supervisors, managers

Time

Fifteen to forty-five minutes

Handouts, Materials, and Equipment

- Paper and pencils for each participant
- A flip chart and markers

Procedure

1. Introduce the activity by noting how we all have made excuses at some time in our lives. Say that such excuses have the potential to interfere with teamwork and that this activity is designed to increase awareness of how excuses can decrease group cohesion.

2. Ask participants to form small groups of three to five members, give everyone paper and a pencil, and ask them to work as a group to list the top excuses people make that interfere with positive outcomes.

3. After groups are finished making their lists, ask each group to select *one* of the excuses and to generate three suggestions for eliminating, preventing, or reducing the possibility of having that particular excuse. Put the following example on the flip chart:

Excuse for not completing task—no time.

Suggestions for eliminating, preventing, or reducing the possibility of people not having enough time: (a) assign priorities to tasks, (b) ensure that all resources needed to deal with a task are available in a timely manner, and (c) allow extra time for all preceding tasks.

4. After each group has finished making suggestions for eliminating one excuse, have them do the same for two more excuses.

5. Have groups list some of their excuses and ways to eliminate or reduce them. Write them on the flip chart. Look for common themes in what they say and point them out. Explain that people often make excuses when they feel that they cannot control the outcome or methods.

Discussion

Lead a discussion, asking for examples of what can be brought under their control and what cannot. Have people think of ways to gain control of their jobs. Bring out that the more excuses group members make for not getting things done, the more difficult it is for any group to cooperate and work together as a team. As a result, group cohesion and productivity are both likely to suffer.

Variation

Have the groups think of the most ridiculous excuses they can think of and award prizes for the best ones (true or not).

Source
Rick Kirschner

Get on the Soapbox

Objectives

- To demonstrate the importance of having fun while working together
- To increase group energy in a simple way
- To bring people closer to one another

Uses

The activity is excellent for building cooperation in teams.

Audience

Any type of group

Time

Ten to twenty minutes

Handouts, Materials, and Equipment

- One soapbox, crate, or sturdy table that is low to the floor per group
- A watch with a second hand or timer

Procedure

1. Divide the participants into groups of seven to ten each.
2. Give each group a soapbox, crate, or table and tell them that the goal of the activity will be to put as many people as possible on the box for one minute. Tell people not to begin until you give the go-ahead.
3. Tell each group to decide on a plan for how to achieve the goal before they begin. After a few minutes, let them try their ideas (all groups at once) while you time them.

Discussion

Discuss how well the teams worked together. Ask questions such as the following:

How were ideas received? Did people listen to one another?

How did people react to the closeness required to be on the box at the same time?

Can any learnings from this activity be generalized to the remainder of the training course?

Variations

1. Use the activity halfway through a training course when participants need an energizer, but always at the start of a new segment of the program.

2. Try this activity outdoors on a tree stump or fallen log.

Source
Arie Maat

Relationship Map

Objectives

- To help participants understand their fellow team members better
- To assess the relationships among team members and determine if and how they want to change those relationships

Uses

The activity is especially useful with teams that are not getting along.

Audience

Any intact work team

Time Required

Two or more hours

Handouts, Materials, and Equipment

- One copy of the *Relationship Map* for each participant
- One overhead transparency of the *Relationship Map*
- Pens or pencils for participants
- An overhead projector and screen
- Washable transparency markers
- A flip chart and markers

Procedure

1. *Prior to the activity:* Use the *Relationship Map* as a template, filling in the names of team members on the blanks. Add spokes if necessary. Make an overhead transparency of the map and enough copies for each participant.

2. Give each participant a pen or pencil and one copy of the *Relationship Map* you have created. Display the transparency. Give the following directions to the group for filling out the maps, going slowly enough that everyone can follow along:

> Write your own name in the center of the circle.
>
> Cross your name off on the spoke at the outside of the circle and write "team" in its place.
>
> Put a dot on each spoke indicating how close you feel to the person whose name is on that spoke. There are no rules to govern placement of your dots. The closer you feel to the team member, the closer the dot should be to the center of the circle. Some of you may feel close to team members because you are friends socially but rarely work together. Others may feel as if you have a close working relationship with someone, but never socialize and really do not know one another. All elements are important when assessing the closeness of the working relationship.
>
> Next, place a dot on the spoke indicating how close you feel to the team as a whole.
>
> Now go back and evaluate how close you *would like* your working relationship to be with each person and with the team. Put an X on each spoke to indicate this.

3. After each person has filled in his or her map, have participants form pairs to share their maps with one another. Allow five minutes for each member of the pair, and then have people switch partners until everyone has shared with everyone else. (For eight participants, this would take about seventy minutes.) Help the group stay on track by reminding them to switch partners every five minutes and pairs every ten minutes. Post the following questions on the flip chart or overhead to keep everyone on track during the discussions:

> *How close did you rate your working relationship with the person?*
>
> *Why did you rate it this way?*
>
> *How close would you like the working relationship to be?*
>
> *What would help you achieve this?*

4. Be flexible at this point. Have the group take a break, which will give people time to finish conversations while their thoughts and feelings are still fresh.

5. After the group reconvenes, write "Team" in the center of the circle on the overhead transparency. Have everyone tell you where they placed their dots on their team spokes, and put their initials on the overhead at the appropriate places. Use a different color marker to indicate where each person placed his or her X.

Discussion

Discuss first what participants learned from sharing one-on-one. Tell them any of your own observations and ask:

What surprises did you have?

Are some of your relationships already where they need to be?

Which relationships would you like to strengthen? How will you go about this process?

Next discuss the team as a whole. Make any observations you have about the team map on the transparency. Ask for their observations, using the following questions:

Does anyone have another observation about the team map?

Were there any surprises?

What can be done to strengthen relationships within the team that are not as strong as desired?

Variation

This activity can be used in conjunction with the Myers-Briggs© Type Indicator (MBTI) or the Kirton Adaption-Innovation Instrument (KAI) by adding the information to the Relationship Map. If two people have the same indications, such as "thinking" or "introverted," for the MBTI, draw a red line on their maps parallel to the spoke that connects them. Draw a line if the KAI scores of the two people are within twenty points. If both instruments are taken, it is possible to have up to five connecting lines indicating traits in common. This is useful to help people see relationships that may require strengthening. (*Note:* The process of drawing lines on the various maps is time consuming and best done overnight between the first and second days of the session or over lunch with the help of several people.)

Source
Mary K. Wallgren

Relationship Map

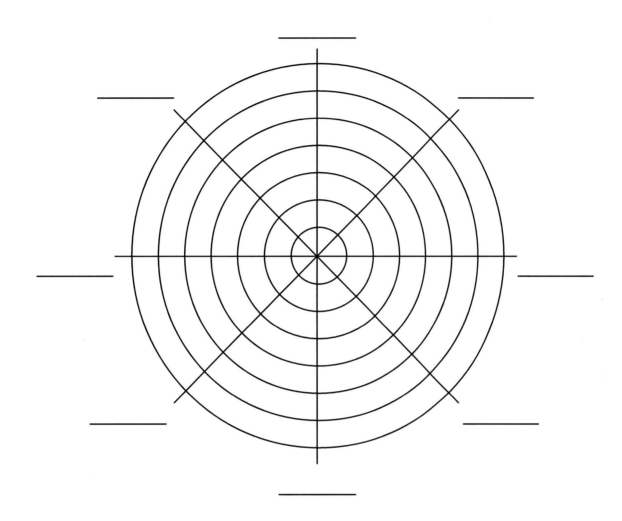

Role Observation Illumination

Objectives

- To explore informal roles and individual behaviors in established groups
- To validate individual perceptions about roles and behaviors in groups
- To encourage discussion about differences in roles within the group

Time

Approximately two hours

Audience

Two or more intact groups with five to eight members each

Materials, Handouts, and Equipment

- One *Role Observation Chart* for each participant
- A pencil for each participant
- A flip chart and markers for each group
- Masking tape
- Separate rooms where group discussion cannot be overheard

Procedure

1. Give each participant one *Role Observation Chart* and a pencil and explain how to use it to identify the roles other group members play by observing their behavior (influence, body language, and message content) in groups. Illustrate this procedure by charting some famous people on the flip chart, such as: George Bush (Active/Team player because of his concern for task and people); Jesse Jackson (Active/Rebel because of his devil's advocate, out-of-the-mainstream role); Bill Cosby (Passive/Team Player because he contributes in many ways); Henry David Thoreau (Passive/Rebel because he was an isolate who wrote about civil disobedience).

2. Divide participants into an even number of groups. Assign one of each pair of groups an actual work-related task to complete or topic to discuss. Encourage participation by using pertinent topics or experiential activities, such as ranking the

characteristics of a well-functioning group, discussing the important stages of group life, or developing a presentation about groups.

3. Assign members of the other group to observe the first group as it goes about the task or discussion. Tell them to identify the quadrant each person is in on the chart. Give the groups twenty minutes to complete the task or discussion while they are being observed.

4. After twenty minutes, have the groups reverse positions and assign a new task or discussion topic.

5. After both rounds are complete, give each group a flip chart and markers and instruct them to adjourn to separate rooms and make two large newsprint *Role Observation Charts,* one for the group they observed and one for their own group.

6. Instruct the members to share their individual observations, explore differences of opinion, and try to reach a consensus for each chart. Encourage the groups to be creative by using different colors, drawings, headings, and presentation styles. Tell them to make any and all modifications that will help explain their observations and give them forty-five minutes to complete the two charts.

7. Bring everyone together and have the groups take turns presenting their charts. Encourage the group that was observed to participate and tape its own chart next to the observation chart, so that the rationale for the ranking and any and all differences in perception can be discussed fully.

Discussion

After each presentation, discuss roles, responsibilities, behaviors, perceptions, and differences between the groups using the following questions:

How do you feel about the observers' chart? Your own group's chart? What are some possible explanations for differences between the charts?

Were there also differences between individuals' perceptions as you created the charts? What sorts of differences emerged?

How does recognizing roles and exploring differences help a group to develop?

Variations

1. Different headings can be used for the axes on the chart.

2. The observing group can act as consultants and use a group-process intervention.

3. A numerical scale can be assigned to the axes.

Source
Gary Wagenheim

Role Observation Chart

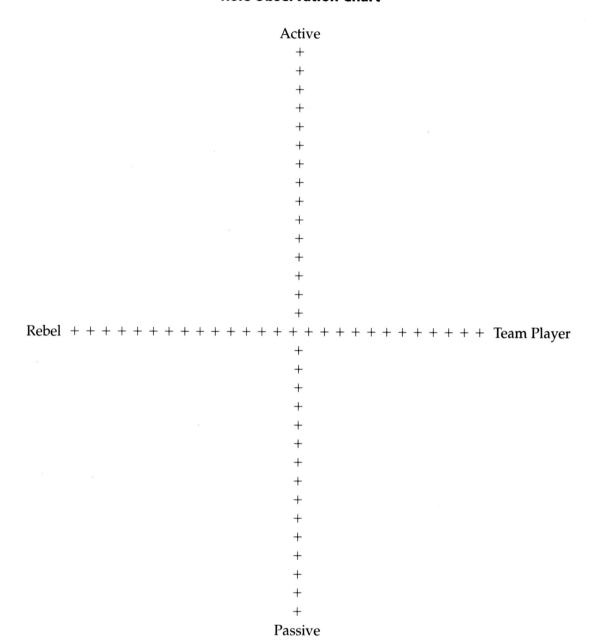

Active

Rebel + Team Player

Passive

Secret Coaches

Objective

- To demonstrate how the facilitation functions of a team are distributed among members

Uses

The activity is excellent for use at the beginning of a team's meeting or can be used at any time when the group seems to be bogged down.

Audience

Any level team

Time

An additional ten minutes during the team's regular meeting

Handouts, Materials, and Equipment

- One 3″ × 5″ index card for each participant
- Pens or pencils for participants

Procedure

1. When the participants arrive, give them index cards and pens or pencils and ask them to write their names on one side of the cards.
2. At the start of the meeting, collect all the cards, turn them upside down, shuffle them, and pass them around the group.
3. Tell each team member to take a card, keeping the name hidden, but making sure it is not his or her own. Tell people to consider the person whose name is on the card to be a secret protégé during the meeting.
4. Tell participants to monitor their protégés secretly and to make sure that they participate appropriately. Tell them to avoid being obvious. Suggest that they make coaching comments to several different people during the meeting (which is a good idea anyway) or that they work through others (another good idea). Give some

examples: "If your protégé is withdrawn, you may encourage him or her by saying, 'What do you think of that idea, Robin?' On the other hand, if the person dominates the discussion, you might ask someone else, 'What do you think of Robin's idea, Dale?'"

5. Now hold the regular meeting, with everybody contributing to the discussion as usual. Take five minutes at the end of the meeting to reveal secret coaches and discuss the experience.

Discussion

Ask participants if the meeting felt different from usual and in what ways. Discuss behavior that was useful and should be carried over into other group meetings. If desired, make a list of desirable and disruptive behaviors for a team meeting and post them in the meeting room for the future.

Source
Sivasailam "Thiagi" Thiagarajan and Raja Thiagarajan

Six Pack

Objectives

- To develop sensitivity to others' feelings
- To sharpen intuitive ability
- To strengthen group cohesion

Uses

This activity is intended to help group members learn to pay attention to one another's feelings and gain better appreciation for one another.

Audience

All levels

Time

Thirty minutes

Handouts, Materials, and Equipment

- Two 3″ × 5″ cards for each participant
- Pencils for participants

Procedure

1. Divide participants into groups of about six people.
2. Distribute two 3″ × 5″ cards and a pencil to each participant.
3. Ask each person to write something on one of the cards about him- or herself that no one else in the small group would know. Give some examples, such as: "When I was ten I broke my arm roller skating." "I always wanted to be an opera singer." "I'm the third daughter of a third daughter." Have someone in each group collect that group's cards when everyone has finished and keep them face down.
4. Tell everyone to list the names of the other people in his or her group on the second card.

5. Ask the person who is holding the first cards collected from each group to turn them over and read them aloud to the other group members.

6. Have members of each group attempt to match the information being read with the list of names and to write the information next to the appropriate name on the list.

7. Have each group record the number of correct matches by each group member and report to the other groups who had the most matches.

Discussion

Have everyone share the clues they used to match information to people. Discuss how picking up on such clues is a good starting point for developing sensitivity toward others and making connections within a group.

Variation

Have groups repeat the activity with new information being shared, either right away or later. This is very helpful for intact groups who will continue to work together.

Source
Doris J. Shallcross

Values

Identifying Cultural Assumptions

Objectives

- To demonstrate that stakeholders may hold different assumptions of where value lies in a new idea or concept
- To increase awareness about the underlying assumptions that shape how people perceive problems and solutions
- To illustrate the importance of understanding the underlying assumptions of others

Uses

This activity can be used for several purposes: For idea generation, it shows participants their unconscious assumptions that shape how they perceive problems and formulate solutions; for team building, it helps participants identify where value lies for members of various cultures and disciplines; and for communication, it shows that one key to successful communication lies in identifying the assumptions held by the recipient so that the communicator can address them.

Audience

Any large or small groups

Time

Twenty minutes or more, depending on group size

Handouts, Materials, and Equipment

- Paper and pencils for participants
- Large sheets of poster board or newsprint and markers for each group
- A flip chart and markers

Procedure

1. Hand out paper and pencils to all participants and instruct the group: "Individually generate a list of words or phrases that express what you personally think are the most interesting and important aspects of (fill in the subject under discussion.)" Give them three to five minutes to generate their lists.

2. *Alternative A:* For large homogeneous groups, separate the group by gender. Give each group poster boards or newsprint and markers and ask each group to produce a common list of words and phrases, based on their individual lists. Give them five minutes to build a group list. (*Note:* If the homogeneous group encompasses a large age range, divide it into age groups in ten-year increments, such as teen to twenty-five, twenty-six to thirty-five, thirty-six to forty-five, forty-six to fifty-five, and fifty-six to sixty-five, etc.)

   Alternative B: For multi-disciplinary teams, separate the groups by discipline. Management groups should be divided into upper and middle management. Give the groups poster boards or newsprint and markers and ask each group to produce a common list of words and phrases, based on their individual lists. Give them five minutes to build a group list.

3. Now give the groups ten more minutes to identify and agree on patterns in what they see as most important about the topic; in other words, what they value most about the session. Post the results on the flip chart for all to see.

Discussion

Ask participants to describe how they identified value by comparing and contrasting the results from working individually or in a group. Ask questions such as:

What words were common to all lists? What concepts are common to all lists? What shared assumptions do they indicate?

Do any of the words and phrases imply intrinsic or extrinsic motivation? What motivation do you hold in common with your groups?

Are the words and phrases reflective of the individual or of the group? How do they reflect individual or group values?

Do any words and phrases focus around certain processes or results? Which ones? Why do you suppose that is true?

Source
J. G. O'Boyle

Values Roll Call

Objectives

- To identify personal values of group members
- To set boundaries for nonthreatening and appropriate discussion in a training session, workplace, or group
- To assess the similarities and diversity of participants' values

Uses

Use the activity when dissimilar attitudes, beliefs, and/or values threaten productivity in a group, for diversity training, or to assess an audience prior to giving a speech or seminar.

Audience

Any intact work group

Time

Forty-five to sixty minutes

Handouts, Materials, and Equipment

- A large whiteboard or flip chart and markers

Procedure

1. Briefly discuss the difference between obvious demographic diversity and more subtle psychographic (individual personality traits) diversity.
2. Ask participants to discuss ways that their own values shape the way they communicate with others.
3. Have each participant call out one value that is important to him or her. Write each word or concept on the whiteboard as it is mentioned.
4. Discuss each word on the whiteboard and combine similar concepts or erase those that not everyone can agree with. The final list should represent the values and attitudes of the entire group.

Discussion

Discuss the final list using the following questions:

How might holding similar or dissimilar values affect your communication with others?

Are you similar or dissimilar to other group members? Is this positive or negative for you?

Does perceived similarity with others reduce your apprehension about working with them? Why or why not?

How can differing viewpoints be used constructively in problem solving?

Will having done this activity shape future communication within your work group in any way? Is this positive or negative?

What have you learned from this activity?

Variation

Ask the participants to write the list of values on a sheet of paper and refer to it during future diversity training or back on the job.

Source
Melinda M. Morris

Value Valuation

Objectives

- To create awareness of work environment values
- To demonstrate how an abstract concept such as values can be made more concrete
- To facilitate understanding of the concept of values

Uses

The activity is especially useful for diversity training or team building.

Audience

All levels, any size group

Time

Twenty minutes

Handouts, Materials, and Equipment

- Several sheets of paper and pencils for each participant

Procedure

1. Distribute paper and pencils and ask each person to draw a square approximately two inches by two inches.

2. Now ask each person to draw a small cube, about the same size as the square.

3. When they are done, ask: "What is the difference between the two?" (*Possible answer:* the cube has depth.)

4. Next have everyone draw a small circle about two inches in diameter. Now ask each person to create the illusion of depth using shading to add a three-dimensional effect.

5. Instruct the participants to draw a vase, a cylinder, and a target.

6. Ask, "How can you create depth in each of these objects?" (*Answer:* shading) "How can you approximate light and darkness in a drawing?" (*Answer:* use black and white.) Point out that white and black represent contrasts that can be used to create depth.

7. Ask, "If objects contain too much gray, how would you differentiate the variations of tones? In other words, What could you do to define the object itself?" (*Answer:* by making them darker or lighter).

8. Have the participants outline the objects they have drawn with dark black lines or white lines. Note how doing this brings out definition and the shape in the objects.

Discussion

Discuss correlations that exist between this activity and clarifying values in the workplace. Use the following questions to focus the discussion:

What correlation exists between value in art and value judgments in the workplace? What examples can you think of?

How can you bring definition to an idea that has too many "shades of gray"?

Think of some recent idea you or someone else had. How could you use contrasts to make it more workable?

Source
Janice Kilgore

Why? Why? Why?

Objectives

- To help participants better understand their core values
- To encourage teams to develop and sustain team values

Uses

The activity can be used for values training, diversity training, or team building.

Audience

All levels of teams in groups of three to seven

Time

Twenty to thirty minutes

Handouts, Materials, and Equipment

- Post-it® Notes (or index cards) and narrow-line markers for each participant
- Paper and a pencil for each participant
- A large, smooth wall
- One flip chart and markers for each group

Procedure

1. Have participants form small groups of three to seven members each and hand out paper, a pencil, Post-it® Notes and narrow-line markers to each person.

2. Ask participants to write down, individually, on the Post-it® Notes, their "purpose" at work, one purpose per note. Tell them not to think in terms of a job description but in terms of "what you are supposed to do," that is, the missions they fulfill. If they ask for clarification, provide only general information and reiterate, "What is it you are supposed to do?"

3. Ask, in turn, "What is the meaning you derive from your work?" "What significance does it hold for you?" "What significance do you think your work holds for others?" "Why is your work important?" Have participants also put these answers on the Post-it® Notes, one answer per note.

4. Ask, "How does what you do fit in with other people in your team?" "How does what you do fit with the larger organization?" "How does it fit with society in general?" Follow the same procedure as before.

5. Have the participants place their Post-it® Notes, by group, on a large, smooth wall or on separate sheets of flip-chart paper.

6. Instruct them to organize the notes for their groups into "affinity groups" (similar categories). Give examples, such as categories pertaining to "helping other people," "making money," "empowering subordinates," or "improving efficiency." Tell them to label each category and place their notes under it.

7. After all groups have determined their categories and placed their notes accordingly, tell them to examine each affinity group and extract the group values represented by that category. Give each group a flip chart and markers and tell them to post their group values on it. (*Note:* Most, if not all, of their values will be represented by the affinity group labels.)

8. Have each group use the values listed to: (a) re-evaluate their personal values and develop a personal work mission statement on a sheet of paper and then (b) develop a mission statement for the group (or modify an existing one if needed) on the flip chart.

Discussion

Pull the groups together for discussion. Point out that values are at the core of all of our beliefs and attitudes. Use the following questions to debrief the activity:

What personal insights did you gain?

Were you aware of all the values associated with your work?

How did this activity affect the way you look at your job? Your team? Your organization? If so, in what way?

Does your new mission statement accurately reflect how you see yourself and your team? Why or why not?

How can you use what you have learned to improve yourself and your job?

Source
Arthur VanGundy

About the Editor

Arthur B. VanGundy, Ph.D., is Professor of Communication at the University of Oklahoma and president of VanGundy & Associates, a creativity and innovation consulting firm. He has twenty-two years' experience in higher education and idea-generation training and facilitation. His academic degrees are from Ohio Wesleyan University (B.A.), Miami University–Ohio (M.S.), and The Ohio State University (Ph.D.).

Dr. VanGundy is considered a pioneer for his work on idea-generation techniques. He has written nine books on creativity and problem solving, as well as two major revisions, including *Techniques of Structured Problem Solving* (1981, 1988), *Training Your Creative Mind* (1982), *108 Ways to Get a Bright Idea* (1983), *Managing Group Creativity* (1984), *Idea Power* (1992), and *Brain Boosters for Business Advantage* (1995).

Dr. VanGundy specializes in facilitating brainstorming retreats for new products and processes. His facilitation and training clients include: Air Canada, Cabot Corporation, Carrier Corporation, Eveready Battery, Hershey Foods Corporation, and Xerox.

He has developed two award-winning idea-generation aids: The Product Improvement CheckList (PICL) and Circles of Creativity. Dr. VanGundy is a member of the Innovation Network, writes the *Creativity in Action* newsletter for the Creative Education Foundation, and is on the Advisory Council of the Galileo Idea Group.

Arthur B. VanGundy, Ph.D.
428 Laws Drive
Norman, OK 73072-3851
Phone: 405-447-1946
Fax: 405-447-1960
E-mail: avangundy@aol.com

About the Authors

Deanna Berg, Ed.D., is president of Innovation Strategies International, an Atlanta-based consulting firm that specializes in innovation, change, and team building. She is known for her creative and highly interactive approaches to helping people and organizations move beyond accustomed ways of thinking to discover powerful new ideas.

Deanna Berg, Ed.D.
5196 Corners Drive
Dunwoody, GA 30338-4305
Phone: 770-351-5080
Fax: 770-351-5081
E-mail: Deanna@profitplay.comsx

Leslie Berger, a principal at Idea Resources, Inc., specializes in generating creative product and marketing breakthroughs for Fortune 1000 companies such as Kraft, S.C. Johnson Wax, Dow, and the Darden Restaurant Group. Her background is in marketing and advertising at two of the world's largest advertising agencies, Leo Burnett and J. Walter Thompson. Ms. Berger has training in Synectics, Edward De Bono, and Osborn-Parnes idea-generating technologies.

Leslie Berger
Idea Resources, Inc.
40 East Oak Street
Chicago, IL 60611
Phone: 847-835-7878
Fax: 847-835-7744
E-mail: ideaglen@aol.com

Robert Alan Black, Ph.D., is an independent consultant and professional speaker who specializes in speaking, training, and facilitation, with an emphasis on the enhancement and application of creative thinking in the workplace through development of skills in coordinating, communicating, collaborating, and creating. Dr. Black has extensive experience with business, industry, educational, and government-sector clients.

Robert Alan Black, Ph.D.
RAB, Inc./Creating and Leading Services
P.O. Box 5805
Athens, GA 30604
Phone: 706-353-3387
Fax: 706-369-1400
E-mail: imcre8ng@uga.cc.uga.edu

Merry C. Buchanan is a third-year doctoral student in communication at the University of Oklahoma. She teaches courses in instructional communication, organizational communication, social change, interpersonal communication, and public speaking at the University of Oklahoma, Oklahoma City University, and the University of Central Oklahoma. She also works as an independent communication consultant.

Merry C. Buchanan
1305 N. Davis Avenue
Oklahoma City, OK 73127
Phone: 405-495-4929
E-mail: mbuchanan@ou.edu

Dr. Marlene Caroselli is the author of *Quality Driven Designs* (Pfeiffer/Jossey-Bass) and two dozen other books dealing with business issues. She is also a frequent contributor to the International Customer Service Association's journal, *The National Business Employment Weekly,* and Stephen Covey's *Executive Excellence.* In addition to directing the Center for Professional Development in Rochester, New York, she conducts training programs for corporate, government, and academic organizations, both nationally and internationally.

Dr. Marlene Caroselli
Director, Center for Professional Development
324 Latona Road
Rochester, NY 14626-2714
Phone: 716-227-6512
Fax: 716-227-6191
E-mail: mccpd@aol.com

Don Crane, founding partner of The Idea Guys, is a creativity coach, trainer, and consultant. Because they believe that the "creativity" of a company's owners, managers, and employees is its most valuable corporate asset, The Idea Guys are sounding the creative wake-up call! They have conducted training and motivational programs for a wide range of organizations, including 3Com, ABC Television Network, CIC/Copley Systems, International Data Group, Massachusetts Society of Certified Public Accountants, Stratus Computer, Suffolk University, and Sun Life of Canada.

Don Crane
The Idea Guys
190 Vincent Road
Dedham, MA 02026
Phone: 617-461-1648
Fax: 617-329-3669
E-mail: IdeaGuyDC@aol.com

Andre de Zanger is director of the Creativity Institute in New York City. He is an international consultant, author, entrepreneur, and seminar leader who has facilitated Creative Innovation projects at AT&T, Western Electric, Ogilvy and Mather, the Department of Defense (DOD), United Technologies, Carrier Corporation, and the Federal Reserve Bank. He has taught at a number of colleges and universities, is the author of *Verti-Think, Paradigm Shifts, Zingers, and Instant Selling,* and has co-authored a chapter on creativity in the *Advertising Manager's Handbook.* Mr. de Zanger is the inventor of an anti-theft auto device and the co-creator of a creativity computer software program.

Andre de Zanger
Director, Creativity Institute
1664 Third Avenue
New York, NY 10128
Phone: 212-289-8856
E-mail: creativityinstitute@juno.com

Maggie Dugan is an international media and creativity consultant based in Paris, France. She has over fifteen years of experience in radio broadcasting as a journalist, marketer, and manager, working at radio stations in the U.S. and Europe. She has attended the Creative Problem Solving Institute in Buffalo, New York, for fourteen years and has been a member of the Institute's faculty since 1993. Ms. Dugan was a leader for the training program, The Effective Facilitator, for Creative Resources, Inc., of Broken Arrow, Oklahoma, and also has worked as a facilitator for the Leadership Training Camp for young adults in Leysin, Switzerland. She works with several European colleagues to lead seminars on creativity and leadership for European student and professional groups.

Maggie Dugan
42 rue des Rosiers
75004 Paris, France
Phone: +(33) 1.42.78.64.96
Fax: +(33) 1.42.78.64.99
E-mail: MDTaz@compuserve.com

Scott Fisher was formerly an intern at Quorum Health Resources while a student in the Department of Human and Organizational Development at Vanderbilt University in Nashville, Tennessee. He graduated from Vanderbilt with a B.S. in organizational development with an emphasis on leadership and organizational effectiveness. He is currently working with Ernst & Young in the Management Consulting Practice in Atlanta, specializing in business change integration and process improvement. He previously worked with DSSA Management and Real Estate Consulting in Chicago.

Scott Fisher
Ernst & Young LLP
660 Peachtree Street
Atlanta, GA 30308-8300
Phone: 404-817-4385
Fax: 404-817-4243

Peter R. Garber is manager of teamwork development for PPG Industries, Inc., Pittsburgh, Pennsylvania. He is the author of nine management books and has contributed activities and learning instruments to the Pfeiffer *Annual* series since 1993.

Peter R. Garber
Manager, Teamwork Development
PPG Industries, Inc.
One PPG Place
Pittsburgh, PA 15272
Phone: 412-434-3417
Fax: 412-434-3490

Dave Gunby is a trainer, facilitator, and the owner of MINDimensions. He specializes in personal creativity and personal effectiveness. Mr. Gunby leads workshops in whole-brain learning and thinking, mind mapping, presentation skills, problem solving and decision making, and Stephen Covey's *Seven Habits of Highly Effective People.* He has spoken to and facilitated learning for thousands of people in corporations, associations, and school systems. He is a member of the National Speakers' Association, the Creative Education Foundation, the Innovation Network, and Toastmasters' International.

Dave Gunby
MINDimensions
2504 Hickory Ridge Drive
Plano, TX 75093
Phone: 972-378-0937
Fax: 972-378-1547
E-mail: dgunby@flash.net

Nance Guilmartin is an Emmy®-award winning marketing communications specialist and leadership coach and now is the director for Essence Marketing. Companies and foundations seek her advice in developing leadership, marketing, and communication breakthroughs to enhance profits and community well-being.

Nance Guilmartin
Essence Marketing
Phone: 508-356-8029
Fax: 508-356-8792

Penny Hampton, M.H.R., is a private training consultant working in the areas of change management, communication, stress management, team engineering, conflict resolution, and leadership. She is founder of GroupMatters, a training company. Her clients include the University of Oklahoma, Oklahoma State University, Metro Tech, EMSA, American Mercury Insurance Company, the Oklahoma Turnpike Authority, the Oklahoma Department of Transportation, United Way, the Oklahoma Foundation for the Disabled, and the CARE Center of Oklahoma City.

Penny Hampton
8812 South Indiana
Oklahoma City, OK 73159
Phone: 405-685-6702
E-mail: grpmttrs@aol.com

Suzanne E. Jonas, Ed.D., L.M.H.C., is a behavioral medicine psychotherapist, educator, researcher, consultant, and trainer. She is president of Music & Medicine, which is devoted to bringing the healing and focusing energies of music and sound to everyone, and on the faculty of the Creative Education Foundation. Dr. Jonas has written a book on the how's and why's of using music and sound: *Take Two Tapes and Call Me in the Morning* and has contributed a chapter, "Music Therapy in Rehabilitation," in the forthcoming book *Physical Medicine and Rehabilitation: The Complete Approach.*

Suzanne E. Jonas
Music & Medicine
5A Meadow Oak Lane
South Deerfield, MA 01373
Phone: 413-665-2390
Fax: 413-268-0399
E-mail: sjonas68@aol.com

M. K. Key, Ph.D., is vice president of the Center for Continuous Improvement at Quorum Health Resources, Inc. She also is an adjunct associate professor at Vanderbilt University. Dr. Key frequently writes and speaks on topics such as leadership, organization development, conflict mediation, and celebration and joy in work.

M. K. Key, Ph.D.
Center for Continuous Improvement
Quorum Health Resources, Inc.
105 Continental Place
Brentwood, TN 27027
Phone: 615-255-0011
Fax: 615-665-1622
E-mail: keyassocs@nashville.com

Janice Kilgore is a multi-talented individual with varied experiences in the professional music world. A dedicated music educator for all levels, she was trained at the University of North Texas and has a master's degree in music education. She is currently working on a doctorate in music education. She has served as a consultant and lecturer since 1987. Her creative approaches to music education promote an enhanced discovering experience for learners.

Janice Kilgore
317 Oak Meadow Lane
Cedar Hill, TX 75104
Phone: 972-291-4361
E-mail: jkkmusik@aol.com

Margaret J. King, Ph.D., is director of Cultural Studies & Analysis, an intelligence research firm that identifies how consumers find and recognize value in products and services. She has published widely on the topics of popular culture, education, and creativity.

Margaret J. King, Ph.D.
Cultural Studies & Analysis
1123 Montrose Street
Philadelphia, PA 19147
Phone: 215-592-8544
Fax: 215-413-9041
E-mail: cultureking@compuserve.com

Dr. Rick Kirschner is a speaker, facilitator, and author of *Talks & Training for Turbulent Times.* He is the owner and creative director of R & R Productions in Ashland, Oregon.

Dr. Rick Kirschner
R & R Productions
P.O. Box 896
Ashland, OR 97520
Phone: 800-884-9444
Phone: 541-488-2992

E-mail: DrRickRnR@usa.net
Webmaster/Web design for the following sites:
Dr. Rick's Website: http://id.mind.net/~drrick
R&R Interactive Website: http://infinite.org/RnR.Productions
AANP Website: http://infinite.org/Naturopathic.Physician
Laughter Site: http://infinite.org/Naturopathic.Physician/Laughter.html

Bill Lazarus, Ph.D., is a consultant specializing in the application of social research methods for the solution of real-world problems. He is an expert in the use of customer research data, as well as internal and third-party databases in conjunction with high-powered analytical tools and breakthrough creativity exercises. Dr. Lazarus has focused on health care, financial services, and information industries. After completing his doctorate in political science from MIT, he joined R. H. Donnelley, where he was responsible for new product development. He also worked as senior vice president at Dun & Bradstreet Plan Services.

Bill Lazarus, Ph.D.
1511 S. Church Avenue
Tampa, FL 33629
Phone: 813-253-5344
Fax: 813-348-4163
E-mail: 76746.537@compuserv.com

Kip L. Lilly provides organization development consulting services for business, professional, trade, and voluntary associations. He specializes in helping organizations successfully adapt to emerging trends. He has nearly two decades of experience in management and public affairs. His areas of expertise include: trend analysis, strategic and operational planning, personnel development, program evaluation, stakeholder relations, and public policy advocacy. He has worked in Botswana, Brazil, China, India, Pakistan, the Philippines, Romania, and Thailand for the Center for International Private Enterprise and has taught for the Institute for Organization Management at universities worldwide. He has conducted over 450 planning sessions and spoken to nearly 1,500 groups. Lilly has a master's degree in urban studies from Occidental College, a bachelor's degree from Carleton College, and has been a CORO Foundation Fellow.

Kip L. Lilly
Foresight Dynamics
165 Western Avenue North
Blair House, Suite 500
St. Paul, MN 55102
Phone: 612-222-7711
Fax: 612-222-4411
E-mail: kiplilly@aol.com

Arie Maat is a consultant working for relief in the city of Deventer, The Netherlands. He has written and published three books on creative thinking, including a number of icebreakers, mental games, eye openers, and energizers.

Arie Maat
E. Tesschenmacherstraat 48
7415 CV Deventer
The Netherlands
Phone: 0570-626068
Fax: 0570-643012

Robert Merritt, Ph.D., is director of Organization Effectiveness Resources. He works with companies to achieve business results by developing effective operational environments. His practice focuses on organizational development, training, and process design.

Robert Merritt
28 St. George Terrace
Bear, DE 19701
Phone: 302-324-0374
E-mail: RMMerritt@aol.com

Judith Morgan is co-director of the Creativity Institute and works as an international creativity consultant. She is a specialist in the psychology of creativity, combining her backgrounds as a sculptor and psychotherapist. Her corporate clients have included The Food Network, Comptom Greaves (India), Citicorp, the Department of Defense (DOD), and the Geyser Advertising Agency. Ms. Morgan teaches in a variety of universities and organizations and is the author of *The Tao of Creativity, Verti-Think,* and *Creativity Therapy,* and has co-authored a chapter on creativity in the *Advertising Manager's Handbook.* She is also the co-creator of a computer program to enhance creativity.

Judith Morgan
Director, Creativity Institute
1664 Third Avenue
New York, NY 10128
Phone: 212-289-8856
E-mail: creativityinstitute@juno.com

Melinda M. Morris, M.A., is an independent training and development consultant who specializes in diversity training, communication dynamics, and public speaking workshops for business and government clients. A former congressional aide and speech writer in Washington, D.C., she is the co-author of two books on public speaking and diversity, and is currently a Ph.D. candidate in communication at the University of Oklahoma.

Melinda M. Morris, M.A.
1809 West Boyd
Norman, OK 73069
Phone: 405-325-0809
Fax: 405-325-7625
E-mail: mmorris@ou.edu

Blair Nickle, M.B.A., M.S.L.S., is a consultant and trainer with Executive Learning, Inc., where she helps organizations plan and implement strategy for the transformation to continual learning and improvement. Ms. Nickle has consulted with a variety of health care organizations. Prior to joining Executive Learning, she served as manager of Corporate Management development for the Tennessee Valley Authority. She holds a B.A. in German and English, a master of science in library science, and a master of business administration.

Blair Nickle, M.B.A., M.S.L.S.
Executive Learning, Inc.
7101 Executive Center Drive, Suite 160
Brentwood, TN 37027
Phone: 615-373-8483
Fax: 615-373-8635
E-mail: blair.nickle@elinc.com

J. G. O'Boyle is senior analyst of Cultural Studies & Analysis, a meta-marketing research firm that identifies how consumers find and recognize value in products and services for corporations and not-for-profit institutions.

J. G. O'Boyle
Cultural Studies & Analysis
1123 Montrose Street
Philadelphia, PA 19147
Phone: 215-592-8544
Fax: 215-413-9041
E-mail: cultureking@compuserve.com

Kristin A. Poppenheimer is a member of the training staff for the Orange County Transportation Authority in Orange, California. She has worked as a designer, trainer, and facilitator in human resource development for the past fifteen years.

Kristin A. Poppenheimer
Orange County Transportation Authority
550 South Main Street
P.O. Box 14184
Orange, CA 92613-1584
Phone: 714-560-5837
Fax: 714-560-5899
E-mail: kpoppenheimer@octa.net

Caroline Portis was formerly an intern at Quorum Health Resources while a student in the Department of Human and Organization Development at Vanderbilt University. She earned her B.S. degree in human and organizational development from Vanderbilt with a minor in health and human services. She is currently working for Hoechst Marion Roussel in Antioch, Tennessee.

Caroline Portis
2302 Hickory Club Drive
Antioch, TN 37013
Phone: 800-321-0855, ext. 9755

Frank Prince is co-founder of the consulting firm, Involvement Systems, Inc., and is recognized as a global leader in the fields of creativity, innovation, and motivation. He is the author of several books, including the best seller from Jossey-Bass/Pfeiffer, *C & the Box*. He serves as a colleague and leader for the Creative Education Foundation and is an adjunct professor for George Fox College and for the Center for Creative Leadership. He conducts the Creative Manager course at Motorola University and the Advanced Leadership Development course at Cambrex University.

Frank Prince
Involvement Systems, Inc.
10635 Buccaneer Point
Frisco, TX 75034
Phone: 972-625-1099
Fax: 972-625-6330
E-mail: fprince@airmail.net

Anne Durrum Robinson is a consultant and owner of Creativity, Communication, and Common Sense in Austin, Texas. She has been an HRD consultant for twenty years. Her many clients have come from business and industry, government, and academia. She has taught workshops and given keynote speeches nationally and internationally on subjects such as creative thinking, Mind Mapping, innovation, creative writing, humor, accelerated learning, and creative aging. She is on the advisory boards for Intuition Network and the American Creativity Association.

Anne Durrum Robinson
2309 Shoal Creek Boulevard
Austin, TX 78705
Phone: 512-472-4412
Fax: 512-832-8386

Doris J. Shallcross, Ed.D., is professor emeritus of the Graduate Program in Creativity at the University of Massachusetts (Amherst) and president of the Shallcross Creativity Institute, which provides consulting in creativity and intuition development for business, education, and other professions as well as summer day camps for children in creativity-related subjects. Dr. Shallcross is the author of four books, including *Teaching Creative Behavior and Intuition: An Inner Way of Knowing,* and is a past president of the Creative Education Foundation Board of Trustees.

Doris J. Shallcross
26 South Main Street
Haydenville, MA 01039
Phone: 413-268-3404
Fax: 413-268-0399
E-mail:shallcro@k12s.phast.umass.edu

Roger J. Syverson has been consulting over thirty years, providing training and guidance to over 150 organizations. His services include product and process development, creativity processes, value analysis, quality function development, and project management. His latest studies are in the field of integrating the flexibility of the creative process and the discipline of the development and improvement process. He teaches at several universities and has published more than one hundred articles. He has degrees in math, physics, and business.

Roger J. Syverson
Professional Value Services
Anthony Lane Offices, Suite 305
2817 Anthony Lane South
St. Anthony, MN 55418
Phone: 612-781-2287
Fax: 612-781-1176

Sivasailam "Thiagi" Thiagarajan has been designing training games and experiential activities for the past twenty-five years. He has designed more than two hundred games and has published thirty books and hundreds of articles on different aspects of human performance technology.

Sivasailam Thiagarajan, Ph.D.
Workshops by Thiagi, Inc.
4423 East Trailbridge Road
Bloomington, IN 47408
Phone: 812-332-1478
Fax: 812-332-5701

Raja Thiagarajan has degrees in astrophysics and computer science. While waiting to decide what to do when he grows up, he too designs games and simulations.

Raja Thiagarajan
Workshops by Thiagi, Inc.
4423 East Trailbridge Road
Bloomington, IN 47408
Phone: 812-332-1478
Fax: 812-332-5701

Robert L. A. Trost is an internationally recognized authority on the relatively new field of Computer-Assisted Brainstorming (CAB). He gives workshops on Structured Brainstorming with the Personal Computer, using a software package he developed, "Operation BrainStorm (OBS) for Windows." He is the initiator of the Global Think Tank (GTT), a worldwide group of creative, well-trained tele-brainstormers in the U.S., Russia, China, and Venezuela, who use OBS to generate and exchange innovative ideas and creative problem solutions via the Internet.

Robert L. A. Trost
CCI, Ltd.
P.O. Box 286
6800 AG Arnhem
Holland
E-mail: 70431.3524@compuserve.com

Arthur VanGundy, Ph.D., is professor of communication at the University of Oklahoma, president of VanGundy & Associates, which specializes in idea generation and new product process innovation, and a senior associate of the Galileo Idea Group. Dr. VanGundy has written nine books on creativity, such as *Idea Power* and *Brain*

Boosters for Business Advantage (Jossey-Bass/Pfeiffer) and has worked with such clients as the Singapore government, Hershey Foods, Rohm & Haas, Johnson Wax, Motorola, Xerox, and Monsanto.

Arthur VanGundy, Ph.D.
VanGundy & Associates
428 Laws Drive
Norman, OK 73072-3851
Phone: 405-447-1946
Fax: 405-447-1960
E-mail: avangundy@aol.com

Gary Wagenheim is an associate professor of Organizational Leadership and Supervision at Purdue University, where he teaches courses in leadership, human resource management, and entrepreneurship. He has published articles in numerous academic journals and currently serves on the board of the Organizational Behavior Teaching Society. He presents workshops for managers and educators at national and international conferences and has consulted with such organizations as Whirlpool, National Association of Electric Distributors, Beechcraft, International Brotherhood of Electrical Workers, Eaton Corporation, and Bethlehem Steel.

Gary Wagenheim, Associate Professor
Department of Organizational Leadership and Supervision
Knoy Hall of Technology
Purdue University
West Lafayette, IN 47907
Phone: 765-494-5613
Fax: 765-496-2519
E-mail: gjwagenheim@tech.purdue.edu

Mary K. Wallgren is currently a senior manager in Human Resources for Procter & Gamble. She coordinates corporate creativity training and consults with groups to apply creative problem solving. She is an experienced and trained consultant, facilitator, and workshop trainer. She has an M.S. degree in creative studies from the State University of New York at Buffalo and is certified in Creative Problem Solving, the KAI Inventory, and the Myers-Briggs© Type Indicator. Ms. Wallgren also represents P&G as a member of both the Association of Managers of Innovation and the PRISM group.

Mary K. Wallgren
The Procter & Gamble Company
Senior Manager, Human Resources
Ivorydale Technical Center, 2N18
5299 Spring Grove Avenue
Cincinnati, OH 45217-1087
Phone: 513-627-8102
Fax: 513-627-7095
E-Mail: wallgren.mk@pg.com

Richard Whelan, M.A., is director of Associated Consultants for Training & Education. He designs, develops, and delivers training programs for conventional classroom settings, as well as computer-based and distance-learning formats. His training programs deal with human resource and mental health issues for both public and private organizations.

Richard Whelan
P.O. Box 5312
Deptford, NJ 08096
Phone: 609-227-4273
Fax: 609-228-9036
E-mail: AssocCnslt@aol.com

Richard G. Wong is manager of training and development at the Orange County Transportation Authority. He also consults on a limited basis and teaches at California State University, Long Beach, and the University of California, Irvine.

Richard G. Wong
Orange County Transportation Authority
550 South Main Street
P.O. Box 14184
Orange, CA 92613-1584
Phone: 714-560-5833
Fax: 714-560-5899
E-mail: rgwong@worldnet.att.net

CPSIA information can be obtained at www.ICGtesting.com
Printed in the USA
BVOW06s0942100514

352954BV00021B/35/P

9 781118 296011